SO-AGF-858

PSYCHE

The Feminine Poetic Consciousness

AN ANTHOLOGY OF
MODERN AMERICAN WOMEN POETS

Edited by

Barbara Segnitz and
Carol Rainey

C34116

PS
589
S4

THE DIAL PRESS
1973

ST. PAUL PUBLIC LIBRARY

Copyright © 1973 by Barbara Segnitz and Carol Rainey
All rights reserved. No part of this book may
be reproduced in any form or by any means without
the prior written permission of the Publisher,
excepting brief quotes used in connection
with reviews written specifically for inclusion
in a magazine or newspaper.

Printed in the United States of America
First printing, 1973

Library of Congress Cataloging in Publication Data

Segnitz, Barbara, 1936–   comp.
Psyche: the feminine poetic consciousness.
1. Women's writings, American. 2. American poetry—20th
century.
I. Rainey, Carol, 1942–   joint comp. II. Title.
PS589.S4   811'.5'08   73–13786

ACKNOWLEDGMENTS

ATWOOD, MARGARET "Game After Supper," "Stories in Kinsman's Park," and "Midwinter, Presolstice" from *Procedures For Underground* by Margaret Atwood, Copyright © 1970 by Oxford University Press (Canadian Branch). "It Is Dangerous To Read Newspapers," "The Landlady," and "The Revenant" from *The Animals in That Country* by Margaret Atwood, Copyright © 1968 by Oxford University Press (Canadian Branch). Reprinted by permission of Atlantic-Little, Brown and Co. and Oxford University Press (Canadian Branch). "They Eat Out," "Their Attitudes Differ," and "After All You Are Quite" from *Power Politics* by Margaret Atwood. Permission, House of Anansi Press, *Power Politics*, 1971.

BRIGHAM, BESMILR "A Dream in Cold," "Heaved from the Earth," and "Rain Sleets Flat" from *Heaved From the Earth* by Besmilr Brigham, Copyright © 1969, 1970, 1971 by Besmilr Brigham. Reprinted by permission of Alfred A. Knopf, Inc. "The State in Indian Language Was Called 'Running Water,'" and "The Sevier County Runaway" first appeared in *PEN: An International Quarterly* and are reprinted with permission.

BROOKS, GWENDOLYN "Riot" from *Riot* by Gwendolyn Brooks, Copyright © 1969 by Gwendolyn Brooks Blakely. Reprinted by permission of Broadside Press. "We Real Cool," Copyright © 1959 by Gwendolyn Brooks Blakely; "The Chicago Picasso," Copyright © 1968 by Gwendolyn Brooks Blakely; and "The Chicago Defender Sends a Man to Little Rock," Copyright ©

1960 by Gwendolyn Brooks Blakely; from *The World of Gwendolyn Brooks*. Reprinted by permission of Harper & Row, Publishers, Inc.

DICKINSON, EMILY #875, "I stepped from Plank to Plank"; #303, "The soul selects her own society"; #338, "I know that He exists"; #280, "I felt a Funeral in my Brain"; #410, "The first Day's Night had come"; #465, "I heard a Fly buzz—when I died"; #476, "I meant to have but modest needs"; #1277, "While we were fearing it, it came"; #1129, "Tell all the Truth but tell it slant"; #870, "Finding is the first act"; #744, "Remorse—is Memory—awake"; #670, "One need not be a Chamber—to be Haunted"; #640, "I cannot live with you"; #609, "I years had been from Home"; #520, "I started Early —Took my Dog." Reprinted by permission of the publishers and the Trustees of Amherst College from Thomas H. Johnson, Editor, *The Poems of Emily Dickinson*, Cambridge, Mass.: The Belknap Press of Harvard University Press. Copyright, 1951, 1955 by The President and Fellows of Harvard College. #341, "After great pain," Copyright 1929, Copyright © 1957 by Mary L. Hampson. #410, "The First Day's Night had come," Copyright 1935 by Martha Dickinson Bianchi, Copyright © renewed 1963 by Mary L. Hampson. #754, "My life had stood—a loaded gun," Copyright 1929, Copyright © 1957 by Mary L. Hampson. Reprinted by permission of Little, Brown and Company.

EVANS, MARI "The Alarm Clock," "Black jam for dr. negro," "To Mother and Steve," and "Vive Noir!" from *I Am a Black Woman*, published by William Morrow & Company, Copyright © 1970 by Mari Evans. Reprinted by permission of the author.

GIOVANNI, NIKKI "For Saundra" and "Woman Poem" from *Black Judgement*, Copyright © 1968 by Nikki Giovanni. Reprinted by permission of Broadside Press. "Black Power" from *Black Feeling, Black Talk*, Copyright © 1968, 1970 by Nikki Giovanni. Reprinted by permission of William Morrow & Company, Inc.

GOEDICKE, PATRICIA "The Slabs of Her Eyes*," "Sprinkle Me,* Just" (first appeared in *The Expatriate Review*, Fall/

Winter 1972–3), "When He's at His Most Brawling" (first appeared in *The Mediterranean Review*), and "My Mother's/ My/Death/Birthday" (first appeared in *The Iowa Review*, Spring, 1971), all copyright by Patricia Goedicke. Reprinted by permission of the author.

JONG, ERICA   "Aging" and "Bitter Pills for the Dark Ladies" from *Fruits & Vegetables* by Erica Jong, Copyright © 1968, 1971 by Erica Jong. Reprinted by permission of Holt, Rinehart & Winston, Inc.

KIZER, CAROLYN   From *"Pro Femina*: One, Two, and Three," from *Knock Upon Silence* by Carolyn Kizer, Copyright © 1963 by Carolyn Kizer. Reprinted by permission of Doubleday & Company, Inc.

LEVERTOV, DENISE   "Song for Ishtar," "The Secret," and "Hypocrite Women" from *O Taste and See*, Copyright © 1962, 1964 by Denise Levertov Goodman. "To the Snake" from *With Eyes at the Back of Our Heads*, Copyright © 1958, 1959 by Denise Levertov Goodman ("To the Snake" was first published in *Poetry*). "The Mutes" and "Stepping Westward" from *The Sorrow Dance*, Copyright © 1966 by Denise Levertov Goodman. "Night on Hatchet Cove" from *The Jacob's Ladder*, Copyright © 1958, 1961 by Denise Levertov Goodman. "Mad Song" and "The Cold Spring" from *Relearning the Alphabet*, Copyright © 1970 by Denise Levertov Goodman. All reprinted by permission of New Directions Publishing Corporation.

LIFSHIN, LYN   "For a Friend," "Nice," "To Poem," and "In Spite of His Dangling Pronoun" from *Black Apples* (Crossing Press) by Lyn Lifshin, Copyright © 1971 by Lyn Lifshin. Reprinted by permission of Crossing Press, Trumansburg, New York. "Downstairs Two Old Lovers Meet and (?) Talk About Me," "Women Like That," and "The Blue Bowl of Plums Invention Or, Not Till The," reprinted by permission of Lyn Lifshin.

LOWELL, AMY   "The Sisters" from *The Complete Poetical Works of Amy Lowell*. Used by permission of Houghton Mifflin Company.

MOORE, MARIANNE "W. S. Landor," Copyright © 1964 by Marianne Moore; "Tell me, Tell me," Copyright © 1960 by Marianne Moore; and "The Mind, Intractable Thing," Copyright © 1965 by Marianne Moore; from *The Complete Poems of Marianne Moore*. (All poems first appeared in *The New Yorker*.) Reprinted by permission of The Viking Press, Inc. "Poetry," "The Frigate Pelican," "Silence," "England," and "To a Steam Roller," Copyright 1935 by Marianne Moore, Copyright renewed 1963 by Marianne Moore and T. S. Eliot. "A Face," Copyright 1951 by Marianne Moore. All from *The Collected Poems of Marianne Moore* and reprinted by permission of The Macmillan Company.

OWENS, ROCHELLE "Let Us Honor Them," "For, Behold The Day Cometh," "The Power of Love," and "Ataturk" from *Salt and Core*, published by Black Sparrow Press, 1968. Poems reprinted by permission of the author.

PIERCY, MARGE "A Cold and Married War" and "Sign" from *Breaking Camp*; "Simple-Song," "I Still Feel You," and "The Organizer's Bogeyman" from *Hard Loving*, Copyright © 1968, 1969 by Marge Piercy. Reprinted by permission of Wesleyan University Press.

PLATH, SYLVIA "The Colossus," Copyright © 1961 by Sylvia Plath. "Mushrooms," Copyright © 1960 by Sylvia Plath. Reprinted from *The Colossus and Other Poems* by Sylvia Plath, by permission of Alfred A. Knopf, Inc., and Olwyn Hughes. "Black Rook in Rainy Weather" from *Crossing the Water* by Sylvia Plath, Copyright © 1971 by Ted Hughes. From *Ariel* by Sylvia Plath: "Tulips," Copyright © 1962 by Ted Hughes; "Lady Lazarus," "The Applicant," "Kindness," and "Daddy," Copyright © 1963 by Ted Hughes; "Ariel," Copyright © 1965 by Ted Hughes. Reprinted by permission of Harper & Row, Publishers, Inc., and Olwyn Hughes.

RICH, ADRIENNE "The Roofwalker," "Double Monologue," and "A Woman Mourned by Daughters" from *Snapshots of a Daughter-In-Law, Poems, 1954–1962* by Adrienne Rich, Copyright © 1956, 1957, 1958, 1959, 1960, 1961, 1962, 1963, 1967 by W. W. Norton & Company, Inc. "I am In Danger—Sir,"

"Necessities of Life," and "Two Songs" from *Necessities of Life, Poems 1962–1965* by Adrienne Rich, Copyright © 1966 by W. W. Norton & Company, Inc. "Women," "Gabriel," and "On Edges" from *Leaflets, Poems 1965–1968* by Adrienne Rich, Copyright © 1969 by W. W. Norton & Company, Inc. All poems reprinted by permission of the publisher.

SEXTON, ANNE "You, Doctor Martin" and "Said the Poet to the Analyst" from *To Bedlam and Part Way Back*, Copyright © 1960 by Anne Sexton. "The Truth the Dead Know," "Housewife," and "The Black Art" from *All My Pretty Ones*, Copyright © 1961, 1962 by Anne Sexton. "Cinderella" from *Transformations*, Copyright © 1971 by Anne Sexton. Reprinted by permission of Houghton Mifflin Company.

SWENSON, MAY "To Make a Play" (first published in *Theatre*, Volume 11, the annual of the Repertory Theater of Lincoln Center, edited by Barry Hyams), Copyright © 1965 by the Repertory Theater of Lincoln Center, Inc., and Hill & Wang, Inc. "Cardinal Ideograms" and "Three Models of the Universe" from *Poems to Solve*, Copyright © 1966 by May Swenson. "At Breakfast," Copyright 1955 by May Swenson; "The Key to Everything," Copyright 1949 by May Swenson; and "The Universe" Copyright © 1963 by May Swenson; from *To Mix With Time*. "How Everything Happens" from *Iconographs*, Copyright © 1969 by May Swenson. Reprinted by permission of Charles Scribner's Sons.

WAKOSKI, DIANE "In Gratitude to Beethoven," from *Inside the Blood Factory* by Diane Wakoski, Copyright © 1962, 1968 by Diane Wakoski. Reprinted by permission of Doubleday & Company, Inc. "The Magician," "A Poet Recognizing the Echo of the Voice," and "In Place of a Phone Call to Arabia" from *The Magellanic Clouds* by Diane Wakoski, Copyright © 1970 by Diane Wakoski. Reprinted by permission of Black Sparrow Press.

WYLIE, ELINOR "Let No Charitable Hope," Copyright 1932 by Alfred A. Knopf, Inc., Copyright renewed 1960 by Edwina C. Rubenstein. "Preference," "This Hand," and "Full Moon," Copyright 1932 by Alfred A. Knopf, Inc., Copyright renewed

1960 by Edwina C. Rubenstein. "Nonsense Rhyme," Copyright
1929 by Alfred A. Knopf, Inc., Copyright renewed 1957 by
Edwina C. Rubenstein. "Sanctuary," Copyright 1921 by Alfred
A. Knopf, Inc., Copyright renewed 1949 by William Rose
Benét. All poems reprinted from *Collected Poems of Elinor
Wylie* by permission of Alfred A. Knopf, Inc.

Two of the charges most frequently levelled against poetry by women are lack of range— in subject matter, in emotional tone—and lack of a sense of humor. And one could, in individual instances among writers of real talent, add other aesthetic and moral shortcomings: the spinning-out; the embroidering of trivial themes; a concern with the mere surfaces of life—that special province of the feminine talent in prose—hiding from the real agonies of the spirit; refusing to face up to what existence is; lyric or religious posturing; running between the boudoir and the altar, stamping a tiny foot against God; or lapsing into a sententiousness that implies the author has reinvented integrity; carrying on excessively about Fate, about time; lamenting the lot of the woman; caterwauling; writing the same poem about fifty times, and so on.

—THEODORE ROETHKE,
from "The Poetry of Louise Bogan"
from *On the Poet and His Craft:
Selected Prose of Theodore Roethke*,
edited by Ralph J. Mills,
reprinted by permission of
the University of Washington Press.

I am obnoxious to each carping tongue
Who says my hand a needle better fits.
A poet's pen all scorn I should thus wrong;
For such despite they cast on female wits,
If what I do prove well, it won't advance—
They'll say it's stolen, or else it was by chance.

—ANNE BRADSTREET, "The Prologue"

Taking us by and large, we're a queer lot
We women who write poetry. And when you think
How few of us there've been, it's queerer still.
I wonder what it is that makes us do it,
Singles us out to scribble down, man-wise,
The fragments of ourselves. Why are we
Already mother-creatures, double-bearing,
With matrices in body and in brain?

—AMY LOWELL, "The Sisters"

From Sappho to myself, consider the fate of women.
How unwomanly to discuss it! Like a noose or an albatross
    necktie
The clinical sobriquet hangs us: cod-piece coveters.
Never mind these epithets; I myself have collected some
    honeys.

—CAROLYN KIZER, from "Pro Femina"

Jus' remember you got no rights. Anything go wrong
they gonna roun' you up & howl "Poetess!"
(sorta like "Nigra!") then kick the shit outa you
sayin': You got Natural Rhythm (28 days)
so why you wanna mess aroun'?

—ERICA JONG, "Bitter Pills for the Dark Ladies"

INTRODUCTION

This is an age which poetry speaks to, and this is an age which recognizes the feminine consciousness. Reason enough for an anthology of this sort. Since, in the past, women poets have been absorbed into the mainstream of poetry, we thought that separating them and looking at them as a group might yield a new perspective. We were especially intrigued with the fact that, beginning with Sappho, the woman poet has provoked an uneasy response. Even Amy Lowell admitted, "We're a queer lot / We women who write poetry." Yet the contemporary poet Carolyn Kizer contends that women poets are the real "custodians of the world's best-kept secret:/ Merely the private lives of one-half of humanity." So we especially looked for reasons why and how women's lives are secret, hoping to uncover patterns of motif and image which would illuminate the "queer" business of being both a woman and a poet—"mother-creatures, double-bearing,/ With matrices in body and in brain."

Certain problems presented themselves. We considered a comprehensive survey, but we also wished to correct what we felt was a distorted view of women poets, due to the overanthologizing of some figures and the neglect of others. Moreover, we felt it necessary to confront and banish the much-maligned image of the Lady Poet, a mythic creature envisioned as sucking cigars in a "mist of chiffon" and tastefully masturbating a limited vision. While Roethke's harsh criteria actually describe any poet of second or lesser rate, certainly the Lady Poet exists. She still receives a lot of recognition by appreciators of the adolescent, clubwoman, or domestic schools of verse. But we have rejected her, since she is imitative of aesthetic traditions and cultural values and too often conforms to an image, seemingly preferred by male editors, of the soft and romantic amateur. Thus the omission of several figures with respectable reputations, such as Anne Bradstreet, Phillis Wheatley, Amy Lowell, H. D., Sara Teasdale, and Edna Millay.

The anthology, then, is not an historical survey, but concentrates on ten women whom we consider to be major poets, i.e., good, serious, and original: Emily Dickinson, Elinor Wylie, Marianne Moore, Gwendolyn Brooks, May Swenson, Denise Levertov, Anne Sexton, Adrienne Rich, Sylvia Plath, and Margaret Atwood. In addition, we have included a briefer introduction to many newer or younger poets who suggest provocative directions. Because of length we have limited ourselves to American poets, cheating only a bit to include a personal discovery, Margaret Atwood, a Canadian. Finally, while the contents of the anthology do reveal fascinating insights into the "condition of women" and women poets, our criterion for including specific poems was simply quality; and our discussions of individual poets are intended only to point out what we feel are relevant connections.

It is essential that this anthology begin with Emily Dickinson, for she articulates the primal concerns which haunt the feminine consciousness: existential isolation, confusion about identity, conflicting realities. While obviously these concerns illustrate the general modern consciousness as much as they do the poetry of women, Emily Dickinson expresses a special point of view typical of the woman poet: a private, personal voice and almost solipsistic vision, an overly modest opinion of her own worth, a conflict between passivity and rebellion against the male-oriented universe, and the assumption that poetry is perhaps the only medium through which one can live a genuine life. Emily Dickinson's psyche itself is particularly appealing to women, for while emotionally she is hypersensitive and vulnerable, her mind is critical and highly self-conscious.

Emily Dickinson is acutely aware of her existential position. Faced with the loss of God as the protective father figure, she envisions herself as a child, who has been "swindled." As the loss of God brings with it the failure of all other identifying securities, including that of language, the abandoned child must rescue herself. For Emily Dickinson, rescue meant forging new definitions for herself and her world. This is readily apparent in merely the format of so many of her beginning lines: "Remorse—is Memory—awake," "My Life had stood—a Loaded Gun." Her great strength lies in the paradox of an almost naïve approach to reality, coupled with a sophisticated control of language. Her brilliant metaphors pierce through the lies, illusions, and veils which confuse reality and resound in the reader's consciousness with the ring of truth.

Adrienne Rich's tribute, "I am in Danger—Sir," captures Emily Dickinson's integrity by acknowledging her to be one

> for whom the word was more
> than a symptom—
> a condition of being.

The poem ends:

> you chose
> silence for entertainment,
> chose to have it out at last
> on your own premises.

Definition on one's own premises. This is the key to the value Emily Dickinson holds for women poets, for the dominant idea unifying the poetry of women is that of defining, or more precisely redefining, themselves and their world more realistically. This reevaluation is necessary because in the past the nature of woman, her modes of perception, and her sphere of engagement have been narrowly and comfortably defined for her. The woman poet experiences an alienating disjuncture between her perceptions of reality and those of the world. She must also cope with the loneliness which results from the lack of community among women themselves, because they lack the confidence to trust or share their perceptions. But there is a more crucial issue involved. Society allows a man's vocation to assume chief priority in his life. He may identify himself as poet first, while his social roles of husband or father assume a secondary psychological importance. But for a woman to adopt this attitude seems to imply a certain selfishness, a shirking of obligations, or a distortion of femininity. Too often a self-destructive frustration and guilt results from trying to do justice to all the conventional functions expected of women and still honor the creative necessity. The alternative seems to demand that the woman poet reject her feminine roles entirely.

In redefining herself and her world, the woman poet's chief confrontation is with a masculine consciousness which has become synonymous with the human consciousness. Initially we considered calling this anthology *Eve's Eye*, a title which turned out to be significantly inappropriate. For we discovered that in searching for mythic ancestresses, women poets reject images glorified by the male imagination, such as Aphrodite, Helen, and Eve— those dual-natured archetypes of Beauty, virgin/seducers, and purveyors of man's joy and destruction. Instead, they find their psychological ties with such figures as Leda, Cassandra, and Lot's wife—all victims of the gods or society, struggling to comprehend their circumstances and to express themselves. They also speak more often through the voice of the child than through the personas of mother or lover, perhaps because society enforces a childlike passivity and dependence on women. Like children, they are uncertain of the future and want to know not only Who am I? but more important, Who am I to become?

Thus the present title, *Psyche*, seems more appropriate since it is the Greek word for both "soul" and "mind." But also, in legend, Psyche was a bit of an upstart, a "new woman" so to speak, with great curiosity and determination. Because of her strange new beauty, she aroused the jealousy of Aphrodite, who set her to all sorts of difficult labors before she could be reunited with Eros, her male counterpart.

Concerned as women are with their relationships to the male, women poets, like women fiction writers, rarely portray convincing male characters. The male figure—whether God, father, husband or lover—emerges as remote and abstract. While this fact applies to the majority of women poets, a significant group avoids altogether the sphere of human relationships. In the poetry of most women the male is usually conceived as an inscrutable symbol of power, with an elusive control over their lives. Perhaps this attitude is the aftermath of the Puritan foundations of our society: the human male has come to absorb the psychological attributes of the Puritan God. This struggle against the authority symbol helps to explain other prevalent themes in the poetry of women, such as parental conflict with both father and mother. Also, the sizable representation of "women" poems implies an intuitive blood tie between these victims of society which transcends other relationships.

In this poetry of redefinition there is a pervading tone of frustration. Yet the qualities women perceive to be thwarted in their lives are only those which would allow them to be more fully themselves: honesty, spirit, creativity, transcendence, autonomous power, and most important, the freedom to know and to realize their individuality and full potential.

Two groups of Emily Dickinson's heirs can be distinguished. The first, more subjective group includes Elinor Wylie, Sylvia Plath, Anne Sexton, Adrienne Rich, Margaret Atwood, and more peripherally, Denise Levertov. These poets attempt to resolve the dilemma of existence by reconciling their inward and outward experience. The quest for personal definition and also for transcendence begins with the self, with the emotions. The second group —Marianne Moore, May Swenson, and another poet not included in this collection, Elizabeth Bishop—emphasizes the mind more than the emotions, and is less autobiographical. For them, language is the starting point, the tool by which to order the world. To capture reality is to name it, to fix it with the apt description or definition. If the first group asks Who am I? the second group asks What is it? Perhaps the same question; only the perspective is reversed.

Emerging from the same austere Puritan environment as Emily Dickinson, Elinor Wylie is in many ways her direct descendant. Her poetry reveals a similar conflict between the Romantic seeker and the New England nun, similar problems with the Puritan God and cultural definition, and a like directness of form and metaphor. However, Elinor Wylie is not the lost child, but the fully mature and worldly woman attempting to reconcile her complexities and to comprehend her own nature.

She best describes herself in "Full Moon":

> There I walked, and there I raged;
> The spiritual savage caged
> Within my skeleton. . . .

"Sanctuary," which also illustrates her great fear of being "walled up" and deadened by life, reveals that she feels trapped, not only by her human limitations, but more especially by the particular restrictions placed on women. Alone and apart from life, she is alternately rebellious and resigned. As she says in "Let No Charitable Hope,"

> I was, being human, born alone;
> I am, being woman, hard beset;
> I live by squeezing from a stone
> The little nourishment I get.

In "Nonsense Rhyme," she cries, ". . . beware the nothing-much/ And welcome madness and the most!" but what really characterizes Elinor Wylie is an ironic vision which controls these yearnings for excess. Still, she strikingly prefigures the position of Sylvia Plath, whose rage for transcendence finally breaks loose in self-destructive fury, and whose notorious "Daddy" must stand as the final condemnation of the Puritan God/father cage.

Sylvia Plath's poetry demands much from the reader, yet the logic behind her imaginative leaps and metaphoric associations is psychologically and aesthetically inevitable. Despite her obvious agony, she is never self-pitying and always darkly witty and ironic toward herself. Lately, she has become a culture heroine: the mad high priestess of the death cult and a martyr to the women's liberation cause. But to interpret her thus, or to regard her as a "confessional" poet is to misrepresent her. One actually learns little of the circumstances of her life from her poems, although obviously many were inspired from specific experiences. For example, one might miss entirely the fact that "Ariel" is about riding her horse.

The point is that the experience of Sylvia Plath's private inward world was far more vivid and meaningful than the events of her life. While extremely sensitive to her environment, her psychological detachment from the people and occasions in her poems illustrates her desire to escape from or neutralize the threatening pressures which even a benign bouquet of tulips could exert. For her primary identity was always that of the poet, that pure essence of creative energy which is the true subject of "Ariel." No definitions of being imposed by society approached the reality of that. As she grimly stated in one of her last poems, "The blood jet is poetry,/ There is no stopping it."

Most of her poems intensely juxtapose this desire for transcendent freedom and the earthly "hooks" which restrict it. Her oppressor is the unresponsive and authoritative male consciousness: by extension the rules and conventions of society which crush individuality, warmth, and imagination. In "Daddy," God, father, and husband are chillingly equated with Nazi Panzer Man; in "The Applicant" marriage itself is the villain.

In other poems, all the good intentions of those who love her do not adequately fulfill her great need for a correspondence in life, which she calls, in "Black Rook in Rainy Weather," that "rare, random descent" of the angel. Life is killing her by its complacent insensitivity, but she refuses to be a passive victim, like the Jews with whom she identifies so closely. If death is the only freedom and escape, she will plunge into it—and transcend it. She is Ariel,

> the arrow,
> The dew that flies
> Suicidal, at one with the drive
> Into the red
>
> Eye, the cauldron of morning.

A poet often linked with Sylvia Plath, Anne Sexton is a truer example of the confessional mode. But however much her poems were impelled from a need to work out personal problems as a kind of self-imposed therapy, they have broader psychological and mythic import. It has been noted, for instance, that her poetry catalogues most of the significant events that can happen in a woman's life. Many of her poems are confrontations with the past, in which the classic battles with parents are refought in order to achieve freedom and identity. As she concludes wryly in "Housewife," "A woman *is* her mother./ That's the main thing."

Like Sylvia Plath, Anne Sexton sees the doctor (or psychiatrist) as a surrogate father figure, but especially as a challenger to the artist. "You, Doctor Martin" and "Said the Poet to the Analyst" debate the crucial distinctions between imagination and insanity. Her concern with this issue illuminates the motif of female powerlessness in society. Historically, the only potent sources of female power have been sex and magic. Rejecting the first as cheapened or sentimentalized by our culture, Anne Sexton introduces herself in her new volume, *Transformations*, thus: "The speaker in this case / is a middle-aged witch, me. . . ." Through art, the individual can express ideas the culture might designate as "mad" and has a freedom to speak the truth as he sees it, a freedom traditionally denied to women. And for Anne Sexton, poetry is magic: "Black Art" describes it as "trances and portents," "spells and fetiches."

Perhaps the chief source of power in the poems themselves is their startling frankness. One feels that here is another poet who dares say anything—as one would expect, of course, from a witch. Her colloquial, even jaunty, tone toward vital and painful material is diabolically compelling.

As so much of her earlier poetry informally pricks the cultural myths which mold our sensibilities and attitudes, it is inevitable that her latest mode is the "transformed" fairy tale. In our reading of women poets, we found the fairy tale to be an important childhood influence which eventually must be reconciled with the reality of actual circumstance. Yet Anne Sexton has stated in a recent interview: "[Fairy tales] reach the unconscious very directly . . . I knew they got to the emotions beneath the formal exterior of the ways people around me acted. What I am trying to get at is the undercurrent of intention— the secret of the fairy tale." *Transformations* particularly exposes the lies and illusions of romantic love which have crippled our culture. Her version of Cinderella ends:

> Cinderella and the prince
> lived, they say, happily ever after,
> like two dolls in a museum case
> never bothered by diapers or dust,
> never arguing over the timing of an egg,
> never telling the same story twice,
> never getting a middle-aged spread,
> their darling smiles pasted on for eternity.

Regular Bobbsey Twins.
That story.

In a different manner, the imagination of Margaret At-
wood transforms the world into an original fairy tale,
which is more like a bad dream. In early poems her per-
sona is the child-victim caught in the adult world where
the possibility of destruction lurks just beyond the most
ordinary circumstances. A simple recollection of a child-
hood game of hide and seek may dissolve into terror:

> From the shadows around
> the corner of the house
> a tall man is coming to find us:
>
> He will be an uncle,
> if we are lucky.

But he may be the ogre who will eat up the innocents, or
some menacing beast. Even the "Landlady" becomes a
malignant omnipresence which intimidates her boarders.

Margaret Atwood sees an incomprehensible universe
where distinctions between reality and illusion are arbi-
trary. There are no certainties, no single truths—especially
in human relationships, which she views as sexual and
psychological combat. Existence is precarious, a matter
of luck. To live means to survive, and the symbolic land-
scape of many poems suggests the polar regions.

However, her latest volume, *Power Politics*, demon-
strates a significant shift in point of view. The dominant
motif is still a kind of primitive survival of the fittest.
However, no longer the helpless child fearing evil from
some outside source, she now recognizes her own power
as the artist who can interpret, manipulate, and thus con-
trol experience. But when all situations are viewed as
potential material for art—"Please die I said/ so I can
write about it"—life comes to resemble a rapid series of
movie clichés or absurd games. Most important, the aware-
ness that one creates his own reality, creates people even,

demands a moral confrontation with one's capacity for destruction.

The atmosphere of violence and illusion in Margaret Atwood's poetry may remind one somewhat of the fictional world of Joyce Carol Oates, but the poet's voice is absolutely unique. Even as her imagination expands the grotesque and surreal possibilities of situations, her tone remains quietly rational. And while her identity is fluid and metamorphic—the resource of the survivor—it exerts itself: she talks back. The typical Margaret Atwood ending which one comes to anticipate is, in the early poems, a startling image which shatters the illusion of safety and order. In her latest poems, however, this ending has become an ultimate weapon of survival, a confirmation of her control of chaos: "This is the way it is," she says calmly, "get used to it."

In contrast, there is a sanity and acceptance of life in the poetry of Denise Levertov which reminds one of the attitudes of Zen. To this poet, "life was an honest breath/ taken in good faith." She too is concerned with defining the transcendent experience; yet it is not desperately sought and seized as with Sylvia Plath, but perceived in the smallest situations and embraced as a natural part of the rhythm of life. From her mystical encounter with "The Snake," she returns merely "smiling and haunted, to a dark morning." The ability of her mind to range back and forth in time and space instills a stirring of wonder at the phenomenon of existence in the present moment. Yet while her poems have an atmosphere of mystery and moonlight, quiet and echo, they are firmly anchored to the here and now, to the concrete and the immediate.

Denise Levertov's poetry expresses a broad and compassionate view of life, and her awareness of complexities and multiple perspectives convinces the reader of the justness of her conclusions. "What do I know?" she asks in "The Cold Spring," an assessment of her life at midpoint. The ultimate answer here, as elsewhere, is the "profound unanswered, sustained echo of our unknowing." This tolerance for ambiguity helps to explain the rare balance she seems to achieve among her various roles of poet, woman, and teacher. But she implies that women have a special obligation to contribute their perspective as a kind of corrective to the state of the world. She is aware that in the past women (herself included) have not spoken out as frankly as they might have. She begins a poem:

> Hypocrite women, how seldom we speak
> of our own doubts, while dubiously
> we mother man in his doubt!

The selections in this anthology do not fully represent the scope of Denise Levertov. Her recent volume, *To Stay Alive*, is essentially one long autobiographical and historical document of social awareness from which it was difficult to excerpt portions. It is described by the poet as "a record of one person's inner/outer experience in America during the '60's and the beginning of the '70's." Initiated by her participation in the war resistance movement, it reveals the author as "committed to a solidarity of hope and struggle with the revolutionary young."

This direction only confirms the importance Denise Levertov has from the beginning given to poetry and to the poet's role in his culture. Much of her work attempts to define the poem itself as a living entity. Yet if the nature of poetry finally cannot be defined, reflecting as it does life's mystery, the poet has a vital responsibility, for poetry has a secret power to strengthen human connection, awareness, and moral values. In "The Secret," she feels grateful toward her students for discovering this and for

> assuming there is
> such a secret, yes,
> for that
> most of all.

With a similar sensitivity, the poetry of Adrienne Rich explores the crisis of the modern intellectual "who has thought/ once too often too coldly." Her Hamlet-like persona experiences a disturbing split between intellect and emotions which results in a double consciousness, an awareness of self observing self. What follows from this distance and division is a fragmentation of being, a loss of the sense of self. Knowing too much carries with it the ultimate danger of all reality dissolving before one's eyes; one lives continually "on edges."

The poetry of Adrienne Rich traces the evolution of a crisis which culminates in her disillusionment with the intellectual life, for it is a half-life, a deadened existence. As she says in "The Roofwalkers,"

> A life I didn't choose
> chose me: even
> my tools are the wrong ones
> for what I have to do.

"What I have to do" is to live an integrated and fully human life. A recovery of self must be achieved; the superfluous must be rejected and the "necessities of life" ascertained. Particularly the truth of the body and the emotions must be reasserted: "What/ pure happiness to know/ all our high-toned questions/ breed in a lively animal." If one is by nature a truth-seeker, one must reconcile the balance between "facts" and "ignorant love." Yet finally, "Both serve, and still/ our need mocks our gear."

Facing the premises of her life leads her to reconsider the adequacy of language to communicate in human relationships. "Gabriel," perhaps about a young student, crystallizes the dilemma of the poet when confronted with one of the "lively animals" of the new generation whose ". . . message/ drenches his body." She realizes, "he'd want to kill me/ for using words to name him," and concedes:

> It's true   there are moments
> closer and closer together
> when words stick   in my throat
>   'the art of love'
>   'the art of words'

The conflict in the poetry of Adrienne Rich between the intellect and the emotions is of general significance to women poets, who often are excessive in one direction or the other. This first, more personal group of poets regard themselves as victims of traditional definition in the sense that intellect has been established as masculine and emotion as feminine. In their earlier poetry, a reticence in subject matter and an overreliance on form is apparent. Adrienne Rich has said that, in her own case, this was perhaps an unconscious desire to gain masculine approval, for the intellectual woman can be admired if she denies her sexuality and does not threaten male preconceptions.

But in rebelling against this unrealistic rigidity, and in trying to define a reality which would allow her a whole nature, she may react with understandably excessive subjectivity. This poetry desperately tries to find verbal equivalents to define the intuitively felt experience. Much of it is characterized by intense conflict and psychological suffering, extending Emily Dickinson's obsession with death as the only escape. The name of one of Anne Sexton's volumes, *Live or Die*, puts this crisis in its starkest terms.

However, a second group of poets chooses neither to play the traditional woman's role nor to react against it. Their poetry is affirmative, on the side of life; but in a sense, they are also victimized, for by evading certain issues, they honor traditional definition with their respectability and civilized attitudes. In defining their reality solely on intellectual terms, they tend to exclude their subjective lives from their poetry. While they are concerned with cultural values, they rarely deal directly with personal problems or human relationships. Their poems, rather, evince an awareness of the possibilities and subtleties of language, and analyze the relation of the mind to the world.

Probably the most intellectual of women poets, Marianne Moore deals primarily with the operation of the mind on reality. A great source of pleasure in her poems comes from her agile angles of vision and the fresh perspectives they give. Given her own predilection not to discuss personal matters, anything can be subject matter for poetry, as evidenced in her famous version of "Poetry":

> elephants pushing, a wild horse taking a roll, a tire-
>   less wolf under a
> tree, the immovable critic twitching his skin like a
>   horse that feels a flea, the base-
> ball fan, the statistician—

Much has been made of the range of odd subjects in her poems—pelicans, steamrollers, baseball—yet her real subject is not the object itself, but the way her mind apprehends it. Her aim is to create things visually with as much vividness and precision as possible, but to suggest obliquely their human, metaphoric, or metaphysical significance. When she does deal with abstract concepts, such as poetry or national character (as in "England"), she is aware of the difficulties in defining reality, which so often appears formless and amorphous. She often proceeds negatively, stating what something is not, before intimating very cautiously what it is.

Certainly, one of her main themes is that finally language cannot ever apprehend reality in any adequate sense, for "deepest feeling always shows itself in silence;/ Not in silence, but restraint." And with the romantic problems of personality, ontology, and transcendence which plague the first group, she simply refuses to deal. Her homage to "W.S. Landor" might well be a self-assessment:

> —considering meanwhile
> infinity and eternity,
> he could only say, "I'll
>   talk about them when I understand them."

With regrets and best wishes, Elizabeth Bishop has declined inclusion in this anthology. Her policy of almost forty years has been to refuse to be represented in any anthology devoted entirely to women. As she has stated in a letter, "I simply prefer the sexes mixed." Few women would disagree with this statement as the ultimate goal of the current women's liberation movement, which hopes to bring about a climate in which the sexes can be "mixed" in a more realistic, humane, and just manner. So, since Elizabeth Bishop is a major poet, and since she exemplifies the more intellectual approach to poetry we have discussed, we've decided, after deliberation, to include a discussion of her poetry in hopes that the reader will at some time read or reread her work.

Elizabeth Bishop's well-known "Invitation to Miss Marianne Moore" demonstrates the kinship between the two poets, but her tone is more personal, her approach less intellectual. Many poems seem like letters written home to friends by an intrepid world traveler who fixes the scenes she passes through with a perspicacious eye. While her approach to the visible world may seem less penetrating than Marianne Moore's, she has a special gift for the precise descriptive detail which triggers a recognition in the reader's senses. She too maintains a certain distance from her subjects, but her encounters involve more of an interchange of personality. "The Fish" is a typical Bishop confrontation. "I stared and stared," she says; yet in this process, almost a mythic power struggle between the human and the non-human is taking place. The poem ends with a gesture of admiration on the poet's part—"And I let the fish go."

Elizabeth Bishop is aware that interpretations of reality are largely projections of the idiosyncrasies of one's personality. In reference to the sound of the water against the wharf, she says, "If one were Baudelaire/one could probably hear it turning to marimba music." But being Elizabeth Bishop, she is content to delight in the play of her own complex fancy upon a situation, as in "The Fishhouses," where she finds a kinship with a particular seal on the basis of their mutual interests—"He was inter-

struggle for recognition. For example, "The Chicago Defender" conveys her desire to confirm a purely human connection which transcends the issue of color, and reveals her empathy with the other side. The opening lines demonstrate her typical attitude of thoughtfulness and fairness:

> In Little Rock the people bear
> Babes, and comb and part their hair
> And watch the want ads, put repair
> To roof and latch.

While her latest poems, such as "Riot," have become more politically aggressive (she now publishes exclusively in black presses), one feels her innate love lies with propagating the universal values of art. As poet laureate of Illinois, her poem on the public dedication of "The Chicago Picasso" is an ironic analysis of the American attitude toward art:

> Does man love Art? Man visits Art, but squirms.
> Art hurts. Art urges voyages—
> And it is easier to stay at home,
> The nice beer ready.

The existence of Gwendolyn Brooks points out an interesting phenomenon. With few exceptions, women poets have been very private and concerned with a small radius of existence. One might argue that the experience of their poetry is deep rather than broad, but it is clear they have not felt comfortable speaking out on the big issues or assuming the role of social critic. Perhaps this is because women have not really felt themselves to be a viable part of the public male-oriented world. Things are changing, however. The latest volumes of Denise Levertov and Adrienne Rich do speak out on such issues as the Vietnam War, changing cultural mores, and the Third World struggle; and more and more cultural spokesmen are emerging, particularly among the Black sisters, such as Nikki Giovanni and Mari Evans. The Women's Liberation movement has a strong representative in Marge Piercy, who tackles both the artist's and the woman's relationship to the new politics. And many other young radical women poets are currently publishing in the underground sheets and little magazines.

On a more private and personal level the quest for identity continues to evolve. The poetry of Carolyn Kizer, Patricia Goedicke, and Lyn Lifshin probes the psychological and social myths which condition women, and displays a fascination with dreams and mythic motifs. In her obsession with male power symbols—"Beethoven" and "George Washington"—Diane Wakoski extends the tradition of Emily Dickinson and Sylvia Plath. Forceful and blunt, her poems bombard the reader with rapidly shifting images of surreal intensity.

Re-definition demands that risks be taken, and women have been understandably reluctant to jeopardize their securtiy. But the younger poets have a directness of subject matter and tone that reflects a newfound confidence. Undoubtedly, the recognition of equality between the sexes contributes to this guilt-free and independent spirit. A willingness to take chances with open forms is also apparent; and the frank language of such poets as Rochelle Owens and Erica Jong, with their emphasis on the physical and the sensual, is a welcome counterforce to the reticence and carefulness of the past. Finally, sex has reinforced love in the poetry of women. In this collection only the poetry of Besmilr Brigham considers the elemental ties of human beings to nature, but one assumes this will be another direction.

At any rate, the future looks lively, now that the cage stands empty.

BARBARA SEGNITZ
CAROL RAINEY

CONTENTS

EMILY DICKINSON

I stepped from Plank to Plank   43
The Soul selects her own Society   43
I know that He exists   43
I felt a Funeral, in my Brain   44
The first Day's Night had come   45
I heard a Fly buzz—when I died   45
I meant to have but modest needs   46
After great pain, a formal feeling comes   47
While we were fearing it, it came   48
Tell all the Truth but tell it slant   48
Finding is the first Act   48
Remorse—is Memory—awake   49
One need not be a Chamber—to be Haunted   49
I cannot live with You   50
I Years had been from Home   52
I started Early—Took my Dog   52
My life had stood—a Loaded Gun   53

ELINOR WYLIE

Let No Charitable Hope   57
Preference   57

Nonsense Rhyme   58
Sanctuary   58
This Hand   59
Full Moon   60

MARIANNE MOORE

Poetry   63
To a Steam Roller   64
The Frigate Pelican   64
A Face   66
Silence   66
England   67
W. S. Landor   68
Tell Me, Tell Me   69
The Mind, Intractable Thing   70

GWENDOLYN BROOKS

We Real Cool   75
The Chicago Defender Sends a Man
     to Little Rock   75
Riot   77
The Chicago Picasso   79

MAY SWENSON

At Breakfast   83
The Key to Everything   84
To Make a Play   86
Cardinal Ideograms   87
3 Models of the Universe   88
The Universe   89
How Everything Happens (Based on a study
     of the Wave)   90

DENISE LEVERTOV

To the Snake   95
Song for Ishtar   95
The Secret   96
Hypocrite Women   97
Mad Song   98
Night on Hatchet Cove   98
The Mutes   99
Stepping Westward   100
The Cold Spring   102

BESMILR BRIGHAM

The State in Indian Language Was Called
        "Running Water"   109
The Sevier County Runaway   112
Heaved from the Earth   113
Rain Sleets Flat   114
A Dream in Cold   114

MARI EVANS

The Alarm Clock   121
Black jam for dr. negro   122
To Mother and Steve   123
Vive Noir!   125

CAROLYN KIZER

From Pro Femina   131
        One   131
        Two   132
        Three   133

ANNE SEXTON

You, Doctor Martin   139
The Truth the Dead Know   140
Housewife   141
Said the Poet to the Analyst   141
The Black Art   142
Cinderella   142

ADRIENNE RICH

"I am in Danger—Sir—"   149
Necessities of Life   149
The Roofwalker   151
Women   152
Two Songs   153
Gabriel   154
On Edges   156
Double Monologue   157
A Woman Mourned by Daughters   158

PATRICIA GOEDICKE

Sprinkle Me,* Just   163
When He's at His Most Brawling   164
The Slabs of Her Eyes*   165
My Mother's/My/Death/Birthday   166

SYLVIA PLATH

The Colossus   169
Mushrooms   170
Black Rook in Rainy Weather   171
Ariel   172
Daddy   173

Kindness   176
The Applicant   177
Tulips   178
Lady Lazarus   180

MARGE PIERCY

Simple-song   187
I Still Feel You   187
A Cold and Married War   188
Sign   189
The Organizer's Bogeymen   190

ROCHELLE OWENS

Let Us Honor Them, the Cliches Which Have Got Us
       All by the Throat   195
For, Behold the Day Cometh   198
The Power of Love
       He Wants Shih (Everything)   199
Ataturk   201

DIANE WAKOSKI

In Gratitude to Beethoven   205
In Place of a Phone Call to Arabia   208
The Magician   209
A Poet Recognizing the Echo of the Voice   210

MARGARET ATWOOD

Game After Supper   217
Stories in Kinsman's Park   218

It Is Dangerous To Read Newspapers   219
The Landlady   220
Midwinter, Presolstice   221
The Revenant   222
They Eat Out   223
Their Attitudes Differ   224
After All You Are Quite   225

LYN LIFSHIN

To Poem   229
In Spite of His Dangling Pronoun   229
For a Friend   230
Nice   232
Downstairs Two Old Lovers Meet and (?) Talk
    About Me   233
Women Like That   234
The Blue Bowl of Plums Invention Or,
    Not Till The   235

ERICA JONG

Aging   241
Bitter Pills for the Dark Ladies   243

NIKKI GIOVANNI

For Saundra   247
Black Power   248
Woman Poem   248

BIOGRAPHIES   251

Emily Dickinson

875

I stepped from Plank to Plank
A slow and cautious way
The Stars about my Head I felt
About my Feet the Sea.

I knew not but the next
Would be my final inch—
This gave me that precarious Gait
Some call Experience.

303

The Soul selects her own Society—
Then—shuts the Door—
To her divine Majority—
Present no more—

Unmoved—she notes the Chariots—pausing—
At her low Gate—
Unmoved—an Emperor be kneeling
Upon her Mat—

I've known her—from an ample nation—
Choose One—
Then—close the Valves of her attention—
Like Stone—

338

I know that He exists.
Somewhere—in Silence—
He has hid his rare life
From our gross eyes.

'Tis an instant's play.
'Tis a fond Ambush—
Just to make Bliss
Earn her own surprise!

But—should the play
Prove piercing earnest—
Should the glee—glaze—
In Death's—stiff—stare—

Would not the fun
Look too expensive!
Would not the jest—
Have crawled too far!

280

I felt a Funeral, in my Brain,
And Mourners to and fro
Kept treading—treading—till it seemed
That Sense was breaking through—

And when they all were seated,
A Service, like a Drum—
Kept beating—beating—till I thought
My Mind was going numb—

And then I heard them lift a Box
And creak across my Soul
With those same Boots of Lead, again,
Then Space—began to toll,

As all the Heavens were a Bell,
And Being, but an Ear,
And I, and Silence, some strange Race
Wrecked, solitary, here—

And then a Plank in Reason, broke,
And I dropped down, and down—
And hit a World, at every plunge,
And Finished knowing—then—

410

The first Day's Night had come—
And grateful that a thing
So terrible—had been endured—
I told my Soul to sing—

She said her Strings were snapt—
Her Bow—to Atoms blown—
And so to mend her—gave me work
Until another Morn—

And then—a Day as huge
As Yesterdays in pairs,
Unrolled it's horror in my face—
Until it blocked my eyes—

My Brain—begun to laugh—
I mumbled—like a fool—
And tho' 'tis Years ago—that Day—
My Brain keeps giggling—still.

And Something's odd—within—
That person that I was—
And this One—do not feel the same—
Could it be Madness—this?

465

I heard a Fly buzz—when I died—
The Stillness in the Room

Was like the Stillness in the Air—
Between the Heaves of Storm—

The Eyes around—had wrung them dry—
And Breaths were gathering firm
For the last Onset—when the King
Be witnessed—in the Room—

I willed my Keepsakes—Signed away
What portion of me be
Assignable—and then it was
There interposed a Fly—

With Blue—uncertain stumbling Buzz—
Between the light—and me—
And then the Windows failed—and then
I could not see to see—

476

I meant to have but modest needs—
Such as Content—and Heaven—
Within my income—these could lie
And Life and I—keep even—

But since the last—included both—
It would suffice my Prayer
But just for One—to stipulate—
And Grace would grant the Pair—

And so—upon this wise—I prayed—
Great Spirit—Give to me
A Heaven not so large as Your's,
But large enough—for me—

A Smile suffused Jehovah's face—
The Cherubim—withdrew—

Grave Saints stole out to look at me—
And showed their dimples—too-—

I left the Place, with all my might—
I threw my Prayer away—
The Quiet Ages picked it up—
And Judgment—twinkled—too—
That one so honest—be extant—
It take the Tale for true—
That "Whatsoever Ye shall ask—
Itself be given You"—

But I, grown shrewder—scan the Skies
With a suspicious Air—
As Children—swindled for the first
All Swindlers—be—infer—

341

After great pain, a formal feeling comes— *Miranda after adams death*
The Nerves sit ceremonious, like Tombs—
The stiff Heart questions was it He, that bore,
And Yesterday, or Centuries before?

The Feet, mechanical, go round—
Of Ground, or Air, or Ought—
A Wooden way
Regardless grown,
A Quartz contentment, like a stone—

This is the Hour of Lead—
Remembered, if outlived,
As Freezing persons, recollect the Snow—
First—Chill—then Stupor—then the letting go—-

1277

While we were fearing it, it came— *miranda — death*
But came with less of fear
Because that fearing it so long
Had almost made it fair—

There is a Fitting—a Dismay—
A Fitting—a Despair—
'Tis harder knowing it is Due
Than knowing it is Here.

The Trying on the Utmost
The Morning it is new
Is Terribler than wearing it
A whole existence through.

1129

Tell all the Truth but tell it slant—
Success in Circuit lies
Too bright for our infirm Delight
The Truth's superb surprise
As Lightning to the Children eased
With explanation kind
The Truth must dazzle gradually
Or every man be blind—

870

Finding is the first Act
The second, loss,
Third, Expedition for
the "Golden Fleece"

Fourth, no Discovery—
Fifth, no Crew—

Finally, no Golden Fleece—
Jason—sham—too.

744

Remorse—is Memory—awake—
Her Parties all astir—
A Presence of Departed Acts—
At window—and at Door—

It's Past—set down before the Soul
And lighted with a Match—
Perusal—to facilitate—
And help Belief to stretch—

Remorse is cureless—the Disease
Not even God—can heal—
For 'tis His institution—and
The Adequate of Hell—

670

One need not be a Chamber—to be Haunted—
One need not be a House—
The Brain has Corridors—surpassing
Material Place—

Far safer, of a Midnight Meeting
External Ghost
Than it's interior Confronting—
That Cooler Host

Far safer, through an Abbey gallop,
The Stones a'chase—
Than Unarmed, one's a'self encounter—
In lonesome Place—

Ourself behind ourself, concealed—
Should startle most—
Assassin hid in our Apartment
Be Horror's least.

The Body—borrows a Revolver—
He bolts the Door—
O'erlooking a superior spectre—
Or More—

640

I cannot live with You—
It would be Life—
And Life is over there—
Behind the Shelf

The Sexton keeps the Key to—
Putting up
Our Life—His Porcelain—
Like a Cup—

Discarded of the Housewife—
Quaint—or Broke—
A newer Sevres pleases—
Old Ones crack—

I could not die—with You—
For One must wait
To shut the Other's Gaze down—
You—could not—

And I—Could I stand by
And see You—freeze—
Without my Right of Frost—
Death's privilege?

Nor could I rise—with You—
Because Your Face
Would put out Jesus'—
That New Grace

Glow plain—and foreign
On my homesick Eye—
Except that You than He
Shone closer by—

They'd judge Us—How—
For You—served Heaven—You know,
Or sought to—
I could not—

Because You saturated Sight—
And I had no more Eyes
For sordid excellence
As Paradise

And were You lost, I would be—
Though My Name
Rang loudest
On the Heavenly fame—

And were You—saved—
And I—condemned to be
Where You were not—
That self—were Hell to Me—

So We must meet apart—
You there—I—here—
With just the Door ajar
That Oceans are—and Prayer—
And that White Sustenance—
Despair—

609

I Years had been from Home
And now before the Door
I dared not enter, lest a Face
I never saw before

Stare stolid into mine
And ask my Business there—
"My Business but a Life I left
Was such remaining there?"

I leaned upon the Awe—
I lingered with Before—
The Second like an Ocean rolled
And broke against my ear—

I laughed a crumbling Laugh
That I could fear a Door
Who Consternation compassed
And never winced before.

I fitted to the Latch
My Hand, with trembling care
Lest back the awful Door should spring
And leave me in the Floor—

Then moved my Fingers off
As cautiously as Glass
And held my ears, and like a Thief
Fled gasping from the House—

520

I started Early—Took my Dog—
And visited the Sea—

The Mermaids in the Basement
Came out to look at me—

And Frigates—in the Upper Floor
Extended Hempen Hands—
Presuming Me to be a Mouse—
Aground—upon the Sands—

But no Man moved Me—till the Tide
Went past my simple Shoe—
And past my Apron—and my Belt
And past my Boddice—too—

And made as He would eat me up—
As wholly as a Dew
Upon a Dandelion's Sleeve—
And then—I started—too—

And He—He followed—close behind—
I felt His Silver Heel
Upon my Ankle—Then my Shoes
Would overflow with Pearl—

Until We met the Solid Town—
No One He seemed to know—
And bowing—with a Mighty look—
At me—The Sea withdrew—

754

My Life had stood—a Loaded Gun—
In Corners—till a Day
The Owner passed—identified—
And carried Me away—

And now We roam in Sovreign Woods—
And now We hunt the Doe—

And every time I speak for Him—
The Mountains straight reply—

And do I smile, such cordial light
Upon the Valley glow—
It is as a Vesuvian face
Had let its pleasure through—

And when at Night—Our good Day done—
I guard My Master's Head—
'Tis better than the Eider-Duck's
Deep Pillow—to have shared—

To foe of His—I'm deadly foe—
None stir the second time—
On whom I lay a Yellow Eye—
Or an emphatic Thumb—

Though I than He—may longer live
He longer must—than I—
For I have but the power to kill,
Without—the power to die—

Elinor Wylie

LET NO CHARITABLE HOPE

Now let no charitable hope
Confuse my mind with images
Of eagle and of antelope:
I am in nature none of these.

I was, being human, born alone;
I am, being woman, hard beset;
I live by squeezing from a stone
The little nourishment I get.

In masks outrageous and austere
The years go by in single file;
But none has merited my fear,
And none has quite escaped my smile.

PREFERENCE

These to me are beautiful people;
Thick hair sliding in a ripple;
A tall throat, round as a column;
A mournful mouth, small and solemn,
Having to confound the mourner
Irony in either corner;
The limbs fine, narrow and strong;
Like the wind they walk along,
Like the whirlwind, bad to follow;
The cheekbones high, the cheeks hollow,
The eyes large and wide apart.
They carry a dagger in the heart
So keen and clean it never rankles. . . .
They wear small bones in wrists and ankles.

NONSENSE RHYME

Whatever's good or bad or both
Is surely better than the none;
There's grace in either love or loathe;
Sunlight, or freckles on the sun.

The worst and best are both inclined
To snap like vixens at the truth;
But, O, beware the middle mind
That purrs and never shows a tooth!

Beware the smooth ambiguous smile
That never pulls the lips apart;
Salt of pure and pepper of vile
Must season the extremer heart.

A pinch of fair, a pinch of foul.
And bad and good make best of all;
Beware the moderated soul
That climbs no fractional inch to fall.

Reason's a rabbit in a hutch,
And ecstasy's a were-wolf ghost;
But, O, beware the nothing-much
And welcome madness and the most!

SANCTUARY

This is the bricklayer; hear the thud
Of his heavy load dumped down on stone.
His lustrous bricks are brighter than blood,
His smoking mortar whiter than bone.

Set each sharp-edged, fire-bitten brick
Straight by the plumb-line's shivering length;

Make my marvellous wall so thick
Dead nor living may shake its strength.

Full as a crystal cup with drink
Is my cell with dreams, and quiet, and cool. . . .
Stop, old man! You must leave a chink;
How can I breathe? *You can't, you fool!*

THIS HAND

This hand you have observed,
Impassive and detached,
With joints adroitly curved,
And fingers neatly matched:

Blue-veined and yellowish,
Ambiguous to clasp,
And secret as a fish,
And sudden as an asp:

It doubles to a fist,
Or droops composed and chill;
The socket of my wrist
Controls it to my will.

It leaps to my command,
Tautened, or trembling lax;
It lies within your hand
Anatomy of wax.

If I had seen a thorn
Broken to grape-vine bud;
If I had ever borne
Child of our mingled blood;

Elixirs might escape;
But now, compact as stone,

My hand preserves a shape
Too utterly its own.

FULL MOON

My bands of silk and miniver
Momently grew heavier;
The black gauze was beggarly thin;
The ermine muffled mouth and chin;
I could not suck the moonlight in.

Harlequin in lozenges
Of love and hate, I walked in these
Striped and ragged rigmaroles;
Along the pavement my footsoles
Trod warily on living coals.

Shouldering the thoughts I loathed,
In their corrupt disguises clothed,
Mortality I could not tear
From my ribs, to leave them bare
Ivory in silver air.

There I walked, and there I raged;
The spiritual savage caged
Within my skeleton, raged afresh
To feel, behind a carnal mesh,
The clean bones crying in the flesh.

Marianne Moore

I, too, dislike it; there are things that are important beyond
    all this fiddle.
    Reading it, however, with a perfect contempt for it, one
        discovers in
    it after all, a place for the genuine.
        Hands that can grasp, eyes
        that can dilate, hair that can rise
            if it must, these things are important not because a

high-sounding interpretation can be put upon them but
    because they are
    useful. When they become so derivative as to become
        unintelligible,
    the same thing may be said for all of us, that we
        do not admire what
        we cannot understand: the bat
            holding on upside down or in quest of something to

eat, elephants pushing, a wild horse taking a roll, a tireless
    wolf under
    a tree, the immovable critic twitching his skin like a
        horse that feels a flea, the base-
    ball fan, the statistician—-
        nor is it valid
            to discriminate against 'business documents and

school-books'; all these phenomena are important. One
    must make a distinction however: when dragged into
    prominence by half poets, the result is not poetry,
nor til the poets among us can be
    'literalists of
    the imagination'—above
        insolence and triviality and can present

for inspection, 'imaginary gardens with real toads in them,'
    shall we have
  it. In the meantime, if you demand on the one hand,
  the raw material of poetry in
    all its rawness and
    that which is on the other hand
      genuine, you are interested in poetry.

TO A STEAM ROLLER

The illustration
is nothing to you without the application.
    You lack half wit. You crush all the particles down
      into close conformity, and then walk back and forth
        on them.

Sparkling chips of rock
are crushed down to the level of the parent block.
    Were not "impersonal judgment in aesthetic
      matters, a metaphysical impossibility," you

might fairly achieve
it. As for butterflies, I can hardly conceive
    of one's attending upon you, but to question
      the congruence of the complement is vain, if it exists.

THE FRIGATE PELICAN

Rapidly cruising or lying on the air there is a bird
    that realizes Rasselas's friend's project
  of wings uniting levity with strength. This
    hell-diver, frigate bird, hurricane-
bird; unless swift is the proper word
    for him, the storm omen when
  he flies close to the waves, should be seen

fishing, although oftener
he appears to prefer

to take, on the wing, from industrious crude-winged species,
the fish they have caught, and is seldom successless.
A marvel of grace, no matter how fast his
victim may fly or how often may
turn. The others with similar ease,
slowly rising once more,
move out to the top
of the circle and stop

and blow back, allowing the wind to reverse their direc-
tion—
unlike the more stalwart swan that can ferry the
woodcutter's two children home. Make hay; keep
the shop; I have one sheep; were a less
limber animal's mottoes. This one
finds sticks for the swan's-down dress
of his child to rest upon and would
not know Gretel from Hänsel.
As impassioned Handel—

meant for a lawyer and a masculine German domestic
career—clandestinely studied the harpsichord
and never was known to have fallen in love,
the unconfiding frigate bird hides
in the height and in the majestic
display of his art. He glides
a hundred feet or quivers about
as charred paper behaves—full
of feints; and an eagle

of vigilance. . . . *Festina lente.* Be gay
civilly? How so? "If I do well I am blessed
whether any bless me or not, and if I do
ill I am cursed." We watch the moon rise
on the Susquehanna. In his way,

this most romantic bird flies
to a more mundane place, the mangrove
    swamp to sleep. He wastes the moon.
    But he, and others, soon

rise from the bough and though flying, are able to foil the
        tired
    moment of danger that lays on heart and lungs the
    weight of the python that crushes to powder.

A FACE

"I am not treacherous, callous, jealous, superstitious,
supercilious, venomous, or absolutely hideous":
    studying and studying its expression,
    exasperated desperation
        though at no real impasse,
        would gladly break the glass;

when love of order, ardor, uncircuitous simplicity
with an expression of inquiry, are all one needs to be!
    Certain faces, a few, one or two—or one
    face photographed by recollection—
        to my mind, to my sight,
        must remain a delight.

SILENCE

My father used to say,
"Superior people never make long visits,
have to be shown Longfellow's grave
or the glass flowers at Harvard.
Self-reliant like the cat—
that takes its prey to privacy,
the mouse's limp tail hanging like a shoelace from its
        mouth—

they sometimes enjoy solitude,
and can be robbed of speech
by speech which has delighted them.
The deepest feeling always shows itself in silence;
not in silence, but restraint."
Nor was he insincere in saying, "Make my house your inn."
Inns are not residences.

ENGLAND

with its baby rivers and little towns, each with its abbey or
    its cathedral,
with voices—one voice perhaps, echoing through the tran-
    sept—the
criterion of suitability and convenience: and Italy
with its equal shores—contriving an epicureanism
from which the grossness has been extracted,

and Greece with its goat and its gourds,
the nest of modified illusions: and France,
the "chrysalis of the nocturnal butterfly,"
in whose products mystery of construction
diverts one from what was originally one's object—
substance at the core: and the East with its snails, its emo-
    tional

shorthand and jade cockroaches, its rock crystal and its
    imperturbability,
all of museum quality: and America where there
is the little old ramshackle victoria in the south,
where cigars are smoked on the street in the north;
where there are no proofreaders, no silkworms, no digres-
    sions;

the wild man's land; grassless, linksless, languageless coun-
    try in which letters are written
not in Spanish, not in Greek, not in Latin, not in shorthand,

but in plain American which cats and dogs can read!
The letter *a* in psalm and calm when
pronounced with the sound of *a* in candle, is very notice-
    able, but

why should continents of misapprehension
have to be accounted for by the fact?
Does it follow that because there are poisonous toadstools
which resemble mushrooms, both are dangerous?
Of mettlesomeness which may be mistaken for appetite,
of heat which may appear to be haste,
no conclusions may be drawn.

To have misapprehended the matter is to have confessed
    that one has not looked far enough.
The sublimated wisdom of China, Egyptian discernment,
the cataclysmic torrent of emotion
compressed in the verbs of the Hebrew language,
the books of the man who is able to say,
"I envy nobody but him, and him only,
who catches more fish than
I do"—the flower and fruit of all that noted superiority—
if not stumbled upon in America,
must one imagine that it is not there?
It has never been confined to one locality.

W. S. LANDOR

There
is someone I can bear—
   "a master of indignation . . .
meant for a soldier
   converted to letters," who could

throw
a man through the window,

yet, "tender toward plants," say, "Good God,
the violets!" (below).
   "Accomplished in every

style
and tint"—considering meanwhile
   infinity and eternity,
he could only say, "I'll
   talk about them when I understand them."

TELL ME, TELL ME

      where might there be a refuge for me
         from egocentricity
and its propensity to bisect,
mis-state, misunderstand
         and obliterate continuity?
            Why, oh why, one ventures to ask, set
flatness on some cindery pinnacle
as if on Lord Nelson's revolving diamond rosette?

      It appeared: gem, burnished rarity
         and peak of delicacy—
in contrast with grievance touched off on
any ground—the absorbing
         geometry of a fantasy:
            a James, Miss Potter, Chinese
"passion for the particular," of a
tired man who yet, at dusk,
         cut a masterpiece of cerise—

      for no tailor-and-cutter jury—
         only a few mice to see,
who "breathed inconsistency and drank
contradiction," dazzled
         not by the sun but by "shadowy
            possibility." (I'm referring

to Henry James and Beatrix Potter's Tailor.)
I vow, rescued tailor
      of Gloucester, I am going

    to flee; by engineering strategy—
    the viper's traffic-knot—flee
to metaphysical newmown hay,
honeysuckle, or woods fragrance.
      Might one say or imply T.S.V.P.—
        Taisez-vous? "Please" does not make sense
to a refugee from verbal ferocity; I am
perplexed. Even so, "deference";
      yes, deference may be my defense.

A précis?
    In this told-backward biography
    of how the cat's mice when set free
by the tailor of Gloucester, finished
the Lord Mayor's cerise coat—
    the tailor's tale ended captivity
      in two senses. Besides having told
of a coat which made the tailor's fortune,
it rescued a reader
      from being driven mad by a scold.

THE MIND, INTRACTABLE THING

even with its own ax to grind, sometimes
   helps others. Why can't it help me?

    O imagnifico,
wizard in words—poet, was it, as
Alfredo Panzini defined you?
Weren't you refracting just now
on my eye's half-closed triptych
   the image, enhanced, of a glen—
"the foxgrape festoon as sere leaves fell"

on the sand-pale dark byroad, one leaf adrift
    from the thin-twigged persimmon; again,

        a bird—Arizona
caught-up-with, uncatchable cuckoo
after two hours' pursuit, zigzagging
road-runner, stenciled in black
stripes all over, the tail
    windmilling up to defy me?
You understand terror, know how to deal
with pent-up emotion, a ballad, witchcraft.
    I don't. O Zeus and O Destiny!

Unafraid of what's done,
undeterred by apparent defeat,
you, imagnifico, unafraid
of disparagers, death, dejection,
have out-wiled the Mermaid of Zennor,
    made wordcraft irresistible:
reef, wreck, lost lad, and "sea-foundered bell"—
as near a thing as we have to a king—
    craft with which I don't know how to deal.

Gwendolyn Brooks

WE REAL COOL

> The Pool Players.
> Seven at the Golden Shovel.

We real cool. We
Left school. We

Lurk late. We
Strike straight. We

Sing sin. We
Thin gin. We

Jazz June. We
Die soon.

Brooks sympathetic to human element in racism poverty

THE CHICAGO DEFENDER SENDS A MAN TO LITTLE ROCK

Fall, 1957

In Little Rock the people bear
Babes, and comb and part their hair
And watch the want ads, put repair
To roof and latch. While wheat toast burns
A woman waters multiferns.

Time upholds or overturns
The many, tight, and small concerns.

In Little Rock the people sing
Sunday hymns like anything,
Through Sunday pomp and polishing.

And after testament and tunes,
Some soften Sunday afternoons
With lemon tea and Lorna Doones.

People in Little Rock - human do daily tasks enjoy normal things

I forecast
And I believe
Come Christmas Little Rock will cleave
To Christmas tree and trifle, weave,
From laugh and tinsel, texture fast.

In Little Rock is baseball; Barcarolle.
That hotness in July . . . the uniformed figures raw and im-
      placable
And not intellectual,
Batting the hotness or clawing the suffering dust.
The Open Air Concert, on the special twilight green. . . .
When Beethoven is brutal or whispers to lady-like air.
Blanket-sitters are solemn, as Johann troubles to lean
To tell them what to mean. . . .

There is love, too, in Little Rock. Soft women softly
Opening themselves in kindness,
Or, pitying one's blindness,
Awaiting one's pleasure
In azure
Glory with anguished rose at the root. . . .
To wash away old semi-discomfitures.
They re-teach purple and unsullen blue.
The wispy soils go. And uncertain
Half-havings have they clarified to sures.

In Little Rock they know
Not answering the telephone is a way of rejecting life,
That it is our business to be bothered, is our business
To cherish bores or boredom, be polite
To lies and love and many-faceted fuzziness.

I scratch my head, massage the hate-I-had.
I blink across my prim and pencilled pad.
The saga I was sent for is not down.
Because there is a puzzle in this town.
The biggest News I do not dare

Telegraph to the Editor's chair:
"They are like people everywhere."

The angry Editor would reply
In hundred harryings of Why.

And true, they are hurling spittle, rock,
Garbage and fruit in Little Rock.
And I saw coiling storm a-writhe
On bright madonnas. And a scythe
Of men harassing brownish girls.
(The bows and barrettes in the curls
And braids declined away from joy.)

I saw a bleeding brownish boy. . . .

The lariat lynch-wish I deplored.

The loveliest lynchee was our Lord.

RIOT

> A riot is the language of the unheard.
> —MARTIN LUTHER KING

John Cabot, out of Wilma, once a Wycliffe,
all whitebluerose below his golden hair,
wrapped richly in right linen and right wool,
almost forgot his Jaguar and Lake Bluff;
almost forgot Grandtully (which is The
Best Thing That Ever Happened To Scotch); almost
forgot the sculpture at the Richard Gray
and Distelheim; the kidney pie at Maxim's,
the Grenadine de Boeuf at Maison Henri.

Because the Negroes were coming down the street.

Because the Poor were sweaty and unpretty
(not like Two Dainty Negroes in Winnetka)

and they were coming toward him in rough ranks.
In seas. In windsweep. They were black and loud.
And not detainable. And not discreet.

Gross. Gross. *"Que tu es grossier!"* John Cabot
itched instantly beneath the nourished white
that told his story of glory to the World.
"Don't let It touch me! the blackness! Lord!" he whispered
to any handy angel in the sky.

But, in a thrilling announcement, on It drove
and breathed on him: and touched him. In that breath
the fume of pig foot, chitterling and cheap chili,
malign, mocked John. And, in terrific touch, old
averted doubt jerked forward decently,
cried "Cabot! John! You are a desperate man,
and the desperate die expensively today."

John Cabot went down in the smoke and fire
and broken glass and blood, and he cried "Lord!
Forgive these nigguhs that know not what they do."

THE CHICAGO PICASSO

August 15, 1967

> "Mayor Daley tugged a white ribbon,
> loosing the blue percale wrap. A
> hearty cheer went up as the covering
> slipped off the big steel sculpture that
> looks at once like a bird and a
> woman."
>
> —·Chicago *Sun-Times*

(Seiji Ozawa leads the Symphony.
The Mayor smiles.
And 50,000 See.)

Does man love Art? Man visits Art, but squirms.
Art hurts. Art urges voyages—
and it is easier to stay at home,
the nice beer ready.
    In commonrooms
we belch, or sniff, or scratch.
Are raw.

But we must cook ourselves and style ourselves for Art, who
is a requiring courtesan.
We squirm.
We do not hug the Mona Lisa.
We
may touch or tolerate
an astounding fountain, or a horse-and-rider.
At most, another Lion.

Observe the tall cold of a Flower
which is as innocent and as guilty,
as meaningful and as meaningless as any
other flower in the western field.

May Swenson

AT BREAKFAST

Not quite
spherical
White
Oddly closed
and without a lid

A smooth miracle
here in my hand
Has it slid
from my sleeve?

The shape
of this box
keels me oval
Heels feel
its bottom
Nape knocks
its top

Seated
like a foetus
I look for
the dream-seam

What's inside?
A sun?
Off with its head
though it hasn't any
or is all head no body
a
One

Neatly
the knife scalps it
I scoop out
the braincap
soft
sweetly shuddering

Mooncream
this could be
Spoon
laps the larger
crescent
loosens a gilded
nucleus
from warm pap
A lyrical food

Opened
a seamless miracle
Ate a sun-germ
Good

THE KEY TO EVERYTHING

Is there anything I can do
or has everything been done
or do
you prefer somebody else to do
it or don't
you trust me to do
it right or is it hopeless and no one can do
a thing or do
you suppose I don't
really want to do
it and am just saying that or don't
you hear me at all or what?

You're
waiting for
the right person the doctor or
the nurse the father or
the mother or
the person with the name you keep
mumbling in your sleep
that no one ever heard of there's no one

named that really
except yourself maybe

If I knew what your name was I'd
prove it's your
own name spelled backwards or
twisted in some way the one you
keep mumbling but you
won't tell me your
name or
don't you know it
yourself that's it
of course you've
forgotten or
never quite knew it or
weren't willing to believe it

Then there *is* something I
can do I
can find your name for you
that's the key to everything once you'd
repeat it clearly you'd
come awake you'd
get up and walk knowing where you're
going where you
came from

And you'd
love me
after that or would you
hate me?
no once you'd
get there you'd
remember and love me
of course I'd
be gone by then I'd
be far away

TO MAKE A PLAY

To make a play
is to make people,
to make people do
what you say;

to make real people
do and say
what you make;
to make people make

what you say real;
to make real
people make up
and do what you

make up. What you
make makes people
come and see
what people do

and say, and then
go away and do
what they see—
and see what

they do. Real
people do and say,
and you see and
make up people;

people come to see
what you do.
They see what *they*
do, and they

may go away undone.
You can make
people, or you
can unmake. You

can do or you
can undo. People
you make up make up
and make people;

people come to
see—to see
themselves real,
and they go away

and do what you
say—as if they
were made up,
and wore make-up.

To make a play
is to make
people; to make
people make

themselves; to
make people
make themselves
new. So real.

CARDINAL IDEOGRAMS

0   A mouth.   Can blow or breathe,
        be funnel, or Hello.

1   A grass blade or a cut.

2   A question seated.   And a proud
        bird's neck.

3   Shallow mitten for two-fingered hand.

4   Three-cornered hut
        on one stilt.   Sometimes built
        so the roof gapes.

5   A policeman.   Polite.
        Wearing visored cap.

6   O unrolling,
        tape of ambiguous length
        on which is written the mystery
        of everything curly.

7   A step,
        detached from its stair.

8   The universe in diagram:
        A cosmic hourglass.
        (Note enigmatic shape,
        absence of any valve of origin,
        how end overlaps beginning.)
        Unknotted like a shoelace
        and whipped back and forth,
        can serve as a model of time.

9   Lorgnette for the right eye.
        In England or if you are Alice
        the stem is on the left.

10   A grass blade or a cut
        companioned by a mouth.
        Open?   Open.   Shut?   Shut.

3 MODELS OF THE UNIVERSE

1.
At moment X
the universe began.
It began at point X.
Since then,
through the Hole in a Nozzle,
stars have spewed. An
inexhaustible gush
populates the void forever.

2.
The universe was there
before time ran.
A grain
slipped in the glass:
the past began.
The Container
of the Stars expands;
the sand
of matter multiplies forever.

3.
From zero radius
to a certain span,
the universe, a Large Lung
specked with stars,
inhales time
until, turgid, it can
hold no more,
and collapses. Then
space breathes, and inhales again,
and breathes again: Forever.

What
is it about,
                the universe
                the universe
            about
us stretching out? We within our brains within it think
    we must unspin the laws that spin it. We think
            why because
                    we think
                because.
                Because
                    we think
                    we think
                the universe
            about
        us.
                    But does it think,
                    the universe?
        Then what
            about?
            About
        us? If not, must there be cause
            in the universe?
Must it have laws? And what
                if the universe
            is *not about*
        us? Then what?
                What
                is it about
            and what
                about
                    us?

HOW EVERYTHING HAPPENS (*Based on a study of the Wave*)

                                        happen.
                                    to
                                up
                            stacking
                        is
                    something

When nothing is happening

When it happens
        something
            pulls
                back
                    not
                        to
                            happen.

When
    pulling back   stacking up
                happens
                                has happened.

When it has happened something pulls back while nothing stacks up.

Then nothing is happening.

Then something stacks up pushes forward and happens.

Denise Levertov

TO THE SNAKE

Green Snake, when I hung you round my neck
and stroked your cold, pulsing throat
    as you hissed to me, glinting
arrowy gold scales, and I felt
    the weight of you on my shoulders,
and the whispering silver of your dryness
    sounded close at my ears—

Green Snake—I swore to my companions that certainly
    you were harmless! But truly
I had no certainty, and no hope, only desiring
    to hold you, for that joy,
        which left
a long wake of pleasure, as the leaves moved
and you faded into the pattern
of grass and shadows, and I returned
smiling and haunted, to a dark morning.

SONG FOR ISHTAR

The moon is a sow
and grunts in my throat
Her great shining shines through me
so the mud of my hollow gleams
and breaks in silver bubbles

She is a sow
and I a pig and a poet

When she opens her white
lips to devour me I bite back
and laughter rocks the moon

In the black of desire
we rock and grunt, grunt and
shine

THE SECRET

Two girls discover
the secret of life
in a sudden line of
poetry.

I who don't know the
secret wrote
the line. They
told me

(through a third person)
they had found it
but not what it was
not even

what line it was. No doubt
by now, more than a week
later, they have forgotten
the secret,

the line, the name of
the poem. I love them
for finding what
I can't find,

and for loving me
for the line I wrote,
and for forgetting it
so that

a thousand times, till death
finds them, they may
discover it again, in other
lines

in other
happenings. And for

wanting to know it,
for

assuming there is
such a secret, yes,
for that
most of all.

HYPOCRITE WOMEN

Hypocrite women, how seldom we speak
of our own doubts, while dubiously
we mother man in his doubt!

And if at Mill Valley perched in the trees
the sweet rain drifting through western air
a white sweating bull of a poet told us

our cunts are ugly—why didn't we
admit we have thought so too? (And
what shame? They are not for the eye!)

No, they are dark and wrinkled and hairy,
caves of the Moon . . .   And when a
dark humming fills us, a

coldness towards life,
we are too much women to
own to such unwomanliness.

Whorishly with the psychopomp
we play and plead—and say
nothing of this later.   And our dreams,

with what frivolity we have pared them
like toenails, clipped them like ends of
split hair.

MAD SONG

My madness is dear to me.
I who was almost always the sanest among my friends,
one to whom others came for comfort,
now at my breasts (that look timid and ignorant,
      that don't look as if milk had flowed from them,
      years gone by)
cherish a viper.
        Hail, little serpent of useless longing
that may destroy me,
that bites me with such idle
needle teeth.

I who am loved by those who love me
for honesty,
to whom life was an honest breath
        taken in good faith,
I've forgotten how to tell joy from bitterness.

Dear to me, dear to me,
blue poison, green pain in the mind's veins.
How am I to be cured against my will?

NIGHT ON HATCHET COVE

The screendoor whines, clacks
shut.   My thoughts crackle
with seaweed-seething diminishing
flickers of phosphorus.   Gulp
of a frog, plash
of herring leaping;
        interval;
squawk of a gull disturbed, a splashing;
pause
while silence poises for the breaking
bark of a seal: but silence.

Then
only your breathing. I'll
be quiet too. Out
stove, out lamp, let
night cut the question with profound
unanswer, sustained
echo of our unknowing.

THE MUTES

Those groans men use
passing a woman on the street
or on the steps of the subway

to tell her she is a female
and their flesh knows it,

are they a sort of tune,
an ugly enough song, sung
by a bird with a slit tongue

but meant for music?

Or are they the muffled roaring
of deafmutes trapped in a building that is
slowly filling with smoke?

Perhaps both.

Such men most often
look as if groan were all they could do,
yet a woman, in spite of herself,

knows it's a tribute:
if she were lacking all grace
they'd pass her in silence:

so it's not only to say she's
a warm hole. It's a word

in grief-language, nothing to do with
primitive, not an ur-language;
language stricken, sickened, cast down

in decrepitude. She wants to
throw the tribute away, dis-
gusted, and can't,

it goes on buzzing in her ear,
it changes the pace of her walk,
the torn posters in echoing corridors

spell it out, it
quakes and gnashes as the train comes in.
Her pulse sullenly

had picked up speed,
but the cars slow down and
jar to a stop while her understanding

keeps on translating:
'Life after life after life goes by

without poetry,
without seemliness,
without love.'

STEPPING WESTWARD

What is green in me
darkens, muscadine.

If woman is inconstant,
good, I am faithful to

ebb and flow, I fall
in season and now

is a time of ripening.
If her part

is to be true,
a north star,

good, I hold steady
in the black sky

and vanish by day,
yet burn there

in blue or above
quilts of cloud.

There is no savor
more sweet, more salt

than to be glad to be
what, woman,

and who, myself,
I am, a shadow

that grows longer as the sun
moves, drawn out

on a thread of wonder.
If I bear burdens

they begin to be remembered
as gifts, goods, a basket

of bread that hurts
my shoulders but closes me

in fragrance. I can
eat as I go.

THE COLD SPRING

i

Twenty years, forty years, it's nothing.
Not a mirage; the blink
of an eyelid.

Life is nibbling us with little
lips, circling our knees, our
shoulders.
       What's the difference,
a kiss or a fin-caress. Only sometimes
the water reddens,
we ebb.

Birth, marriage, death, we've had them,
checked them off on our list,
and still stand here

tiptoe on the mud,
half-afloat,
water up to the neck.

It's a big pond.

ii

What do I know?
       Swing of the
       birch catkins,
       drift of
       watergrass,
       tufts of
       green on the
       trees,

(flowers, not leaves,
bearing intricately
little winged seeds
to fly in fall)
and whoever
I meet now,
on the path.
It's not enough.

iii
Biology and the computer—
the speaker implies
we're obsolescent

we who grew up
towards utopias.

In this
amnesia of the heart
I'm wondering,

I almost believe him.
What do I know?
A poem, turn of the head,

some certainty
of mordant delight—
five notes, the return
of the All Day Bird—:

truces, for the new moon
or the spring solstice,
and at midnight the firing resumes,

far away.
It's not real.

We wanted
more of our life to live in us.
To imagine each other.

iv
Twenty years, forty years,
'to live in the present' was a utopia
moved towards

in tears, stumbling, falling,
getting up, going on—
and now the arrival,

the place of pilgrimage curiously
open, not, it turns out,
a circle of holy stones,

no altar, no
high peak,
no deep valley, the world's navel,

but a plain,
only green tree-flowers
thinly screening the dayglare

and without silence—
we hear the traffic, the highway's
only a stonesthrow away.

Is this the place?

v
This is not the place.
The spirit's left it.

Back to that mud my feet felt
when as a child I fell off a bridge
and almost drowned, but rising

found myself dreamily upright,
water sustaining me,
my hair watergrass.

vi
Fishes bare their teeth to our flesh.
The sky's drifting toward our mouths.
Forty years redden the spreading circles.
Blink of an eyelid,
nothing,
obsolete future—

vii
If I should find my poem is deathsongs.
If I find it has ended, when
I looked for the next step.

Not Spring is unreal to me,
I have the tree-flowers by heart.
Love, twenty years, forty years, my life,
      is unreal to me.
I love only the stranger
coming to meet me now
up the path that's pinpricked with
yellow fallen crumbs of pollen.

I who am not about to die,
I who carry my life about with me openly,
health excellent, step light, cheerful, hungry,

my starwheel rolls. Stops
on the point of sight.
Reduced to an eye
I forget what
                  I
was.

Asking the cold spring
what if my poem is deathsongs.

Besmilr Brigham

THE STATE IN INDIAN LANGUAGE
WAS CALLED "RUNNING WATER"

The West Oklahoma Wind

i
a not-quiet touchable air
blows the scant trees, blows the plains of
rock

against the single houses

a little green on the grass, last winter rain
before the heat, drouth after Spring

a long night, sitting in the wind, porch
of loneliness, two women in the house
sleeping. women sleeping
who as children-girls
looked at the wind. their loneliness covers
the un-still air

(so different here. a belly of growth—
surrounded by trees. a poured-over running
green)

birds
sit on the street-light poles, scream
their tails blown—scream at the clouds
that roll with morning. black mass on
black mass that in shape
changes. rolling over the plains
for Arkansas

the wind
blows them hard to the south, banked
on the west. through the openings

a solid light
of moon and not moving cloud above

the witch is out! the
violent old weather witch of storm and
tornado wind

sits in our minds. she has driven the children
in. and the women-children sleep

(the weather vane stands solid; we
drive all day
following the rain)

ii
a restlessness

the wind blew into the child

the two little girls that we wait for on the
weather vane
their feet caught in the wind; and the two

in child-sleep in the room

caught on the same spindle. some movement
we can't see
revolves them. always wanting to get away

the morning wakes them to witches, age;
the night
closes them to dreams

      iii
      the voices of the people are harsh
      as the wind
      their hearts
      hushed and silent as the houses are

before the blackest cloud dips

a bareness of hurled flesh and wood
lies fierce on the plains. spirits of the dead,
a dead race
a Choctaw and Comanche blackness
silent in the rock, riding their horses
                    in dust-cloud and
the straight-down lightning streaks
that touch

the ground, roll with the thunder of
last drums

women in houses, women in teepees
women in the quiet of womanliness and girlness
like soft stones the dirt has been blown away

from, their bodies

(buried in graves
in Arkansas)

buried where the scant brisk trees stand
down by the new cemetery; their fathers
and men

found it hard to dig into the earth with plows

iv
the man who holds the weather vane
has dreams in his eyes

the man who held it, who holds the women
is long dead

(all night in that house
we waited for morning)

THE SEVIER COUNTY RUNAWAY

an ad in the paper, 1843

> two negro slaves
> one old
> an ear cut off—
> the other 'cropped'
>
> color:
> deep black
>
> he took nothing
> his name: BOB
>
> > the young negro
> > left on a horse

an old black man with his ears cut
walking through these bottoms
wading the Costock, river up—
an old black man
sleeping under a big sweet gum

hurrying through the pines
breathing the air i breathe. here

his ear holes listening. i touch the side
of his cut face; i see his black face
crying
the anger in his eyes is dark as the
wolf's. the accusation of his eyes

looks out from the dark yard
of this house. an old black man
dead,

lying deep in the wood, his black body
on the black earth. he is covered in leaves
he does not hear the young man

                    riding, riding

HEAVED FROM THE EARTH

after the tornado, a dead moccasin
nailed to the pole
boards scattered across a pasture

lying fierce crosses
jagged in mud

had flung itself
nail and wood
the square-head animal
hurled also in air

or as it raced in weeds
) water flowing, water falling
impaled
        both the snake and timber
went flying through with wind

coiled, made a coil (they do
immediately from danger or when hurt
and died in a coil
bit itself
in pain of its own defense the poison

                birds
                hurled into yard
                fences
                one with feet tangled gripping
                the open wire, a big Jay

struggling from the water
throwing its fanged head
high at the lightning, silent
in all that thunder

to die by its own mouth
pushing the fire thorns in

RAIN SLEETS FLAT

bending down the huddle sprout grass
lights in puddles between the grass spindles
settles
washing crevices dense into
the bank of graves

the earth is covered with clods and rock
caked over

above
habitat high on the mountain
like some strange shell blown there, thrown
dripping
the cave
its bare opening pours gulped with watery sand

the dead
lie in their brief houses
there is nothing to wake them
they are safe from the wolves

A DREAM IN COLD

the sun eyed fire-macaw sits in a white tree
at corner of the universe

(i

north is the horizontal-line
south lies heat
past the horizon's rim the warm inland bay
a bird with white wings
sleeps
the rivers of melting water
never wake her
she sleeps and dreams

'but i am a bird whose song is cold'

carved bone the sun rims over
an all night long of waking
splintering with sticks like strokes of fire
burns and dazzles
and shoots its high shafts into the drawn
bows of violet
pointed arrows, the frozen wings

            'i am a bird
            whose dream is of heat
            who sings of the cold'

down the blue-curved mountain glacier
white bear fur
swallows under the fish-hut eaves fish nets
        fragile at still windows
fish scales of shimmer ice
falling from ledge to ledge, sails
that plunge circling
surrounded with frozen islands of water

hawkweed and birds—
melting down the blue-cloud mountains
they bring with them
                bells
                the spear bone
and candles from bee's wax

the men hunt for the feather
from the white bird for their arrows

over drift peaks the wind-blown rain

(ii

        'a white bird flying low
        against the white ground'
        (the snow

moves cold above the tundra
its mist heavied up
   in the air suspended

on tipped flint
split-resounding boulders
the thunder
beyond the long flat frozen roll
wolves
the white bear that lapped in cavern falls
pointed,
from swift rain cuts through the sky
from settled natural pyramids of space

drawn from the low ice-free ridges
of grass land

white and glistening
     the full-tip woodline
warm lateral valleys
a jungle of sudden creepers
and fawn-hair aspen

leaving the cave by starlight
a monster of fallen avalanche
smokes over, scented and sulled
brief
the solid melt turns

splendidly down a wild gorge opening of
cliffs

serpents crawling through the dark
the living
have broken into the graves and pulled the dead about

falling like fluffs of stars
a few flakes of
        grass stems and
lark feathers
flocks of simple herd feeding next to
where the sun was
surrounded by fields of winter

it was growing dark
no lamps were allowed
stones hurling plunged into the deep side gullies
the white bird
high on the furtherest boulder

has drawn his shot wings

Mari Evans

THE ALARM CLOCK

Alarm clock
sure sound
loud
this mornin'

remind me of the time
I sat down
in a drug store
with my mind
a way far off

until the girl
and she was small
it seems to me
with yellow hair
a hangin'
smiled up and said
'I'm sorry but
we don't serve
you people
here'
and I woke up
quick
like I did this mornin'
when the
alarm
went off

It don't do
to wake up
quick

BLACK JAM FOR DR. NEGRO

Pullin me in off the corner to wash my face an
cut my fro off turn
my collar
down
when that aint my
thang I
walk heels first
nose round an tilted
up
my ancient
eyes
see your thang
baby
an it aint
shit
your thang
puts my eyes out baby
turns my seeking fingers
   into splintering fists
messes up my head
an I scream you out
your thang
is what's wrong
   an' you keep
   pilin it on rubbin it
   in
   smoothly
   doin it
   to death

what you sweatin
baby
       your guts
puked an rotten
waitin'

to be defended

TO MOTHER AND STEVE

All I wanted
was your
love

when I roiled down
Brewster blew
soft pot clouds on
subs when
I lay in nameless rooms
cold-sweating
horse in nameless arms
crawled
thru white hell owning
no one no one no one save
one purple-bruised soul
pawned
in exchange for
oblivion
    all I wanted
was
your love

not twice but
constantly
I tried
to free you

it was all
such cold shit
then
the last day
of the
last year
of my raw-edged anguish
I was able wearily
at last—
to roll.

(all I wanted
was
your love)
I bought this final
battered gift
(do not refuse—for it
was all
I had)

with my back supported
by the tolerant
arms
of a picket fence and my
legs crumpled crazily in front
and love fell
soft and cold and
covered me in
blanket
like
the one you
tucked around me
centuries
ago and like that
later
gently pulled
across my face
and in this season
of peace and
goodwill and the smell
of cedar
remembered
thru warm yellow
windows—
    all I wanted
and it was more than
I could stand and
more than a thousand passions and
I could not

mainline it
away

    was your
    love

VIVE NOIR!

i
am going to rise
en masse
from Inner City
               sick
            of newyork ghettos
            chicago tenements
      l   a's slums
weary
    of exhausted lands
    sagging privies
    saying yessuh yessah
    yesSIR
    in an assortment
    of geographical dialects i
have seen my last
broken down plantation
even from a
distance
        i
will load all my goods
in '50 Chevy pickups '53
Fords fly United and '66
caddys i
    have packed in
    the old man and the old lady and
    wiped the children's noses
        I'm tired
           of hand me downs

                    shut me ups
                        pin me ins
                            keep me outs
                                messing me over have
                            just had it
                        baby
                    from
                you . . .
i'm
gonna spread out
over America
            intrude
my proud blackness
all
        over the place
                    i have wrested wheat fields
                    from the forests

                    turned rivers
                    from their courses
                    leveled mountains
                    at a word
                    festooned the land with
                    bridges
                            gemlike
                        on filaments of steel
                                moved

        glistening towersofBabel in place
                    like blocks
        sweated a whole
        civilization

            now
                    i'm
        gonna breathe fire
        through flaming nostrils BURN
            a place for

            me

in the skyscrapers and the
schoolrooms on the green
lawns and the white
beaches
                    i'm
gonna wear the robes and
sit on the benches
make the rules and make
the arrests say
who can and who
can't
                    baby you don't stand
                    a
                    chance
i'm
        gonna put black angels
        in all the books and a black
        Christchild in Mary's arms i'm
        gonna make black bunnies black
        fairies black santas black
        nursery rhymes and
                              black
        ice cream
                        i'm
gonna make it a
        crime
            to be anything BUT   black
            pass the coppertone

gonna make white
a twentyfourhour
lifetime
J.O.B.
            an' when all the coppertone's gone . . . ?

Carolyn Kizer

FROM PRO FEMINA

One

From Sappho to myself, consider the fate of women.
How unwomanly to discuss it! Like a noose or an albatross
    necktie
The clinical sobriquet hangs us: cod-piece coveters.
Never mind these epithets; I myself have collected some
    honeys.
Juvenal set us apart in denouncing our vices
Which had grown, in part, from having been set apart:
Women abused their spouses, cuckolded them, even
    plotted
To poison them. Sensing, behind the violence of his
    manner—
"Think I'm crazy or drunk?"—his emotional stake in us,
As we forgive Strindberg and Nietzsche, we forgive all
    those
Who cannot forget us. We *are* hyenas. Yes, we admit it.

While men have politely debated free will, we have
    howled for it,
Howl still, pacing the centuries, tragedy heroines.
Some who sat quietly in the corner with their embroidery
Were Defarges, stabbing the wool with the names of their
    ancient
Oppressors, who ruled by the divine right of the male—
I'm impatient of interruptions! I'm aware there were
    millions
Of mutes for every Saint Joan or sainted Jane Austen,
Who, vague-eyed and acquiescent, worshiped God as a
    man.
I'm not concerned with those cabbageheads, not truly
    feminine
But neutered by labor. I mean real women, like *you*
    and like *me*.

Freed in fact, not in custom, lifted from furrow and
    scullery,
Not obliged, now, to be the pot for the annual chicken,
Have we begun to arrive in time? With our well-known
Respect for life because it hurts so much to come out
    with it;
Disdainful of "sovereignty," "national honor" and other
    abstractions;

We can say, like the ancient Chinese to successive waves of
    invaders,
"Relax, and let us absorb you. You can learn temperance
In a more temperate climate." Give us just a few decades
Of grace, to encourage the fine art of acquiescence
And we might save the race. Meanwhile, observe our
    creative chaos,
Flux, efflorescence—whatever you care to call it!

Two
I take as my theme, "The Independent Woman,"
Independent but maimed: observe the exigent neckties
Choking violet writers; the sad slacks of stipple-faced
    matrons;
Indigo intellectuals, crop-haired and callous-toed,
Cute spectacles, chewed cuticles, aced out by full-time
    beauties
In the race for a male. Retreating to drabness, bad manners
And sleeping with manuscripts. Forgive our transgressions
Of old gallantries as we hitch in chairs, light our own
    cigarettes,
Not expecting your care, having forfeited it by trying to
    get even.

But we need dependency, cosseting and well-treatment.
So do men sometimes. Why don't they admit it?
We will be cows for a while, because babies howl for us,
Be kittens or bitches, who want to eat grass now and then
For the sake of our health. But the role of pastoral heroine

Is not permanent, Jack. We want to get back to the
    meeting.

Knitting booties and brows, tartars or termagants, ancient
Fertility symbols, chained to our cycle, released
Only in part by devices of hygiene and personal daintiness,
Strapped into our girdles, held down, yet uplifted by man's
Ingenious constructions, holding coiffures in a breeze,
Hobbled and swathed in whimsey, tripping on feminine
Shoes with fool heels, losing our lipsticks, you, me,
In ephemeral stockings, clutching our handbags and
    packages.

Our masks, always in peril of smearing or cracking,
In need of continuous check in the mirror or silverware,
Keep us in thrall to ourselves, concerned with our surfaces.
Look at man's uniform drabness, his impersonal envelope!
Over chicken wrists or meek shoulders, a formal,
    hard-fibered assurance
The drape of the male is designed to achieve self-
    forgetfulness.

So, sister, forget yourself a few times and see where it gets
    you:
Up the creek, alone with your talent, sans everything else.
You can wait for the menopause, and catch up on your
    reading.
So primp, preen, prink, pluck and prize your flesh,
All posturings! All ravishment! All sensibility!
Meanwhile, have you used your mind today?
What pomegranate raised you from the dead,
Springing, full-grown, from your own head, Athena?

Three
I will speak about women of letters, for I'm in the racket.
Our biggest successes to date? Old maids to a woman.
And our saddest conspicuous failures? The married
    spinsters

On loan to the husbands they treated like surrogate fathers.
Think of that crew of self-pitiers, not-very-distant,
Who carried the torch for themselves and got first-degree
    burns.
Or the sad sonneteers, toast-and-teasdales we loved at
    thirteen;
Middle-aged virgins seducing the puerile anthologists
Through lust-of-the-mind; barbiturate-drenched Camilles
With continuous periods, murmuring softly on sofas
When poetry wasn't a craft but a sickly effluvium,
The air thick with incense, musk, and emotional blackmail.

I suppose they reacted from an earlier womanly modesty
When too many girls were scabs to their stricken
    sisterhood,
Impugning our sex to stay in good with the men,
Commencing their insecure bluster. How they must have
    swaggered
When women themselves indorsed their own inferiority!
Vestals, vassals and vessels, rolled into several,
They took notes in rolling syllabics, in careful journals,
Aiming to please a posterity that despises them.
But we'll always have traitors who swear that a woman
    surrenders
Her Supreme Function, by equating Art with aggression
And failure with Femininity. Still, it's just as unfair
To equate Art with Femininity, like a prettily-packaged
    commodity
When we are the custodians of the world's best-kept
    secret:
Merely the private lives of one-half of humanity.

But even with masculine dominance, we mares and
    mistresses
Produced some sleek saboteuses, making their cracks
Which the porridge-brained males of the day were too
    thick to perceive,

134

Mistaking young hornets for perfectly harmless
     bumblebees.
Being thought innocuous rouses some women to frenzy;
They try to be ugly by aping the ways of the men
And succeed. Swearing, sucking cigars and scorching the
     bedspread,
Slopping straight shots, eyes blotted, vanity-blown
In the expectation of glory: *she writes like a man!*
This drives other women mad in a mist of chiffon
(one poetess draped her gauze over red flannels, a
     practical feminist).

But we're emerging from all that, more or less,
Except for some lady-like laggards and Quarterly
     priestesses
Who flog men for fun, and kick women to maim
     competition.
Now, if we struggle abnormally, we may almost seem
     normal;
If we submerge our self-pity in disciplined industry;
If we stand up and be hated, and swear not to sleep with
     editors;
If we regard ourselves formally, respecting our true
     limitations
Without making an unseemly show of trying to unfreeze
     our assets;
Keeping our heads and our pride while remaining
     unmarried;
And if wedded, kill guilt in its tracks when we stack up the
     dishes
And defect to the typewriter. And if mothers, believe in the
     luck of our children,
Whom we forbid to devour us, whom we shall not devour,
And the luck of our husbands and lovers, who keep
     free women.

Anne Sexton

YOU, DOCTOR MARTIN

You, Doctor Martin, walk
from breakfast to madness. Late August,
I speed through the antiseptic tunnel
where the moving dead still talk
of pushing their bones against the thrust
of cure. And I am queen of this summer hotel
or the laughing bee on a stalk

of death. We stand in broken
lines and wait while they unlock
the door and count us at the frozen gates
of dinner. The shibboleth is spoken
and we move to gravy in our smock
of smiles. We chew in rows, our plates
scratch and whine like chalk

in school. There are no knives
for cutting your throat. I make
moccasins all morning. At first my hands
kept empty, unraveled for the lives
they used to work. Now I learn to take
them back, each angry finger that demands
I mend what another will break

tomorrow. Of course, I love you;
you lean above the plastic sky,
god of our block, prince of all the foxes.
The breaking crowns are new
that Jack wore. Your third eye
moves among us and lights the separate boxes
where we sleep or cry.

What large children we are
here. All over I grow most tall
in the best ward. Your business is people,
you call at the madhouse, an oracular

eye in our nest. Out in the hall
the intercom pages you. You twist in the pull
of the foxy children who fall

like floods of life in frost.
And we are magic talking to itself,
noisy and alone. I am queen of all my sins
forgotten. Am I still lost?
Once I was beautiful. Now I am myself,
counting this row and that row of moccasins
waiting on the silent shelf.

THE TRUTH THE DEAD KNOW

For my mother, born March 1902, died March 1959
and my father, born February 1900, died June 1959

Gone, I say and walk from church,
refusing the stiff procession to the grave,
letting the dead ride alone in the hearse.
It is June. I am tired of being brave.

We drive to the Cape. I cultivate
myself where the sun gutters from the sky,
where the sea swings in like an iron gate
and we touch. In another country people die.

My darling, the wind falls in like stones
from the whitehearted water and when we touch
we enter touch entirely. No one's alone.
Men kill for this, or for as much.

And what of the dead? They lie without shoes
in their stone boats. They are more like stone
than the sea would be if it stopped. They refuse
to be blessed, throat, eye and knucklebone.

HOUSEWIFE

Some women marry houses.
It's another kind of skin; it has a heart,
a mouth, a liver and bowel movements.
The walls are permanent and pink.
See how she sits on her knees all day,
faithfully washing herself down.
Men enter by force, drawn back like Jonah
into their fleshy mothers.
A woman *is* her mother.
That's the main thing.

SAID THE POET TO THE ANALYST

My business is words. Words are like labels,
or coins, or better, like swarming bees.
I confess I am only broken by the sources of things;
as if words were counted like dead bees in the attic,
unbuckled from their yellow eyes and their dry wings.
I must always forget how one word is able to pick
out another, to manner another, until I have got
something I might have said . . .
but did not.

Your business is watching my words. But I
admit nothing. I work with my best, for instance,
when I can write my praise for a nickel machine,
that one night in Nevada: telling how the magic jackpot
came clacking three bells out, over the lucky screen.
But if you should say this is something it is not,
then I grow weak, remembering how my hands felt funny
and ridiculous and crowded with all
the believing money.

THE BLACK ART

A woman who writes feels too much,
those trances and portents!
As if cycles and children and islands
weren't enough; as if mourners and gossips
and vegetables were never enough.
She thinks she can warn the stars.
A writer is essentially a spy.
Dear love, I am that girl.

A man who writes knows too much,
such spells and fetiches!
As if erections and congresses and products
weren't enough; as if machines and galleons
and wars were never enough.
With used furniture he makes a tree.
A writer is essentially a crook.
Dear love, you are that man.

Never loving ourselves,
hating even our shoes and our hats,
we love each other, *precious, precious.*
Our hands are light blue and gentle.
Our eyes are full of terrible confessions.
But when we marry,
the children leave in disgust.
There is too much food and no one left over
to eat up all the weird abundance.

CINDERELLA

You always read about it:
the plumber with twelve children
who wins the Irish Sweepstakes.
From toilets to riches.
That story.

Or the nursemaid,
some luscious sweet from Denmark
who captures the oldest son's heart.
From diapers to Dior.
That story.

Or a milkman who serves the wealthy,
eggs, cream, butter, yogurt, milk,
the white truck like an ambulance
who goes into real estate
and makes a pile.
From homogenized to martinis at lunch.

Or the charwoman
who is on the bus when it cracks up
and collects enough from the insurance.
From mops to Bonwit Teller.
That story.

Once
the wife of a rich man was on her deathbed
and she said to her daughter Cinderella:
Be devout. Be good. Then I will smile
down from heaven in the seam of a cloud.
The man took another wife who had
two daughters, pretty enough
but with hearts like blackjacks.
Cinderella was their maid.
She slept on the sooty hearth each night
and walked around looking like Al Jolson.
Her father brought presents home from town,
jewels and gowns for the other women
but the twig of a tree for Cinderella.
She planted that twig on her mother's grave
and it grew to a tree where a white dove sat.
Whenever she wished for anything the dove
would drop it like an egg upon the ground.
The bird is important, my dears, so heed him.

Next came the ball, as you all know.
It was a marriage market.
The prince was looking for a wife.
All but Cinderella were preparing
and gussying up for the big event.
Cinderella begged to go too.
Her stepmother threw a dish of lentils
into the cinders and said: Pick them
up in an hour and you shall go.
The white dove brought all his friends;
all the warm wings of the fatherland came,
and picked up the lentils in a jiffy.
No, Cinderella, said the stepmother,
you have no clothes and cannot dance.
That's the way with stepmothers.

Cinderella went to the tree at the grave
and cried forth like a gospel singer:
Mama! Mama! My turtledove,
send me to the prince's ball!
The bird dropped down a golden dress
and delicate little gold slippers.
Rather a large package for a simple bird.
So she went. Which is no surprise.
Her stepmother and sisters didn't
recognize her without her cinder face
and the prince took her hand on the spot
and danced with no other the whole day.

As nightfall came she thought she'd better
get home. The prince walked her home
and she disappeared into the pigeon house
and although the prince took an axe and broke
it open she was gone. Back to her cinders.
These events repeated themselves for three days.
However on the third day the prince
covered the palace steps with cobbler's wax
and Cinderella's gold shoe stuck upon it.

Now he would find whom the shoe fit
and find his strange dancing girl for keeps.
He went to their house and the two sisters
were delighted because they had lovely feet.
The eldest went into a room to try the slipper on
but her big toe got in the way so she simply
sliced it off and put on the slipper.
The prince rode away with her until the white dove
told him to look at the blood pouring forth.
That is the way with amputations.
They don't just heal up like a wish.
The other sister cut off her heel
but the blood told as blood will.
The prince was getting tired.
He began to feel like a shoe salesman.
But he gave it one last try.
This time Cinderella fit into the shoe
like a love letter into its envelope.

At the wedding ceremony
the two sisters came to curry favor
and the white dove pecked their eyes out.
Two hollow spots were left
like soup spoons.

Cinderella and the prince
lived, they say, happily ever after,
like two dolls in a museum case
never bothered by diapers or dust,
never arguing over the timing of an egg,
never telling the same story twice,
never getting a middle-aged spread,
their darling smiles pasted on for eternity.
Regular Bobbsey Twins.
That story.

Adrienne Rich

Old Mortality -

Miranda ... ... about believe
... ... just as wonderful

... ...
for husband

... to be free of past specify

...
Meanan - ... of ... bird of
... ... for
death - ...

"I AM IN DANGER—SIR—"

"Half-cracked" to Higginson, living,
afterward famous in garbled versions,
your hoard of dazzling scraps a battlefield,
now your old snood

mothballed at Harvard
and you in your variorum monument
equivocal to the end—
who are you?

Gardening the day-lily,
wiping the wine-glass stems,
your thought pulsed on behind
a forehead battered paper-thin,

you, woman, masculine
in single-mindedness,
for whom the word was more
than a symptom—

a condition of being.
Till the air buzzing with spoiled language
sang in your ears
of Perjury

and in your half-cracked way you chose
silence for entertainment,
chose to have it out at last
on your own premises.

NECESSITIES OF LIFE

Piece by piece I seem
to re-enter the world: I first began

a small, fixed dot, still see
that old myself, a dark-blue thumbtack

pushed into the scene,
a hard little head protruding

from the pointillist's buzz and bloom.
After a time the dot

begins to ooze. Certain heats
melt it.
            Now I was hurriedly

blurring into ranges
of burnt red, burning green,

whole biographies swam up and
swallowed me like Jonah.

Jonah! I was Wittgenstein,
Mary Wollstonecraft, the soul

of Louis Jouvet, dead
in a blown-up photograph.

Till, wolfed almost to shreds,
I learned to make myself

unappetizing. Scaly as a dry bulb
thrown into a cellar

I used myself, let nothing use me.
Like being on a private dole,

sometimes more like kneading bricks in Egypt.
What life was there, was mine,

now and again to lay
one hand on a warm brick

and touch the sun's ghost
with economical joy,

now and again to name
over the bare necessities.

So much for those days. Soon
practice may make me middling-perfect, I'll

dare inhabit the world
trenchant in motion as an eel, solid

as a cabbage-head. I have invitations:
a curl of mist steams upward

from a field, visible as my breath,
houses along a road stand waiting

like old women knitting, breathless
to tell their tales.

THE ROOFWALKER

for Denise

Over the half-finished houses
night comes. The builders
stand on the roof. It is
quiet after the hammers,
the pulleys hang slack.
Giants, the roofwalkers,
on a listing deck, the wave

of darkness about to break
on their heads. The sky
is a torn sail where figures
pass magnified, shadows
on a burning deck.

I feel like them up there:
exposed, larger than life,
and due to break my neck.

Was it worth while to lay—
with infinite exertion—
a roof I can't live under?
—All those blueprints,
closings of gaps,
measurings, calculations?
A life I didn't choose
chose me: even
my tools are the wrong ones   *to live a integrated & fully*
for what I have to do. ——>   *human life*
I'm naked, ignorant,
a naked man fleeing
across the roofs
who could with a shade of difference
be sitting in the lamplight
against the cream wallpaper
reading—not with indifference—
about a naked man
fleeing across the roofs.

WOMEN

for C.R.G.

My three sisters are sitting
on rocks of black obsidian.
For the first time, in this light, I can see who they are.

152

I sit in the bare apartment
reading
words stream past me   poetry
twentieth-century rivers
disturbed surfaces   reflecting clouds
reflecting wrinkled neon
but clogged   and mostly
nothing alive left
in their depths

The angel is barely
speaking   to me
Once in a horn of light
he stood   or someone like him
salutations in gold-leaf
ribboning from his lips
Today again   the hair streams
to his shoulders
the eyes reflect   something
like a lost country   or so I think
but the ribbon has reeled itself
up
    he isn't giving
or taking any shit
We glance miserably
across the room   at each other

It's true   there are moments
closer and closer together
when words stick   in my throat
                    'the art of love'
                    'the art of words'
I get your message Gabriel
just   will you stay looking
straight at me
awhile longer

ON EDGES

When the ice starts to shiver
all across the reflecting basin
or water-lily leaves
dissect a simple surface
the word 'drowning' flows through me.
You built a glassy floor
that held me
as I leaned to fish for old
hooks and toothed tin cans,
stems lashing out like ties of
silk dressing-gowns
archangels of lake-light
gripped in mud.

Now you hand me a torn letter.
On my knees, in the ashes, I could never
fit these ripped-up flakes together.
In the taxi I am still piecing
what syllables I can
translating at top speed like a thinking machine
that types out 'useless' as 'monster'
and 'history' as 'lampshade'.
Crossing the bridge I need all my nerve
to trust to the man-made cables.

The blades on that machine
could cut you to ribbons
but its function is humane.
Is this all I can say of these
delicate hooks, scythe-curved intentions
you and I handle? I'd rather
taste blood, yours or mine, flowing
from a sudden slash, than cut all day
with blunt scissors on dotted lines
like the teacher told.

DOUBLE MONOLOGUE

To live illusionless, in the abandoned mine-
    shaft of doubt, and still
mime illusions for others? A puzzle
    for the maker who has thought
once too often too coldly.

Since I was more than a child
    trying on a thousand faces
I have wanted one thing: to know
    simply as I know my name
at any given moment, where I stand.

How much expense of time and skill
    which might have set itself
to angelic fabrications! All merely
    to chart one needle in the haymow?
Find yourself and you find the world?

Solemn presumption! Mighty Object
    no one but itself has missed,
what's lost, if you stay lost? Someone
    ignorantly loves you—will that serve?
Shrug that off, and presto!—

the needle drowns in the haydust.
    Think of the whole haystack—
a composition so fortuitous
    it only looks monumental.
There's always a straw twitching somewhere.

Wait out the long chance, and
    your needle too could get nudged up
to the apex of that bristling calm.
    Rusted, possibly. You might not want
to swear it was the Object, after all.

Time wears us old utopians.
    I now no longer think
"truth" is the most beautiful of words.
    Today, when I see "truthful"
written somewhere, it flares

like a white orchid in wet woods,
    rare and grief-delighting, up from the page.
Sometimes, unwittingly even,
    we have been truthful.
In a random universe, what more

exact and starry consolation?
    Don't think I think
facts serve better than ignorant love.
    Both serve, and still
our need mocks our gear.

A WOMAN MOURNED BY DAUGHTERS

Now, not a tear begun,
we sit here in your kitchen,
spent, you see, already.
You are swollen till you strain
this house and the whole sky.
You, whom we so often
succeeded in ignoring!
You are puffed up in death
like a corpse pulled from the sea;
we groan beneath your weight.
And yet you were a leaf,
a straw blown on the bed,
you had long since become
crisp as a dead insect.
What is it, if not you,
that settles on us now
like satin you pulled down

over our bridal heads?
What rises in our throats
like food you prodded in?
Nothing could be enough.
You breathe upon us now
through solid assertions
of yourself: teaspoons, goblets,
seas of carpet, a forest
of old plants to be watered,
an old man in an adjoining
room to be touched and fed.
And all this universe
dares us to lay a finger
anywhere, save exactly
as you would wish it done.

Patricia Goedicke

SPRINKLE ME,* JUST

Sprinkle me, just
sow me
with any amount
of powdered sugar, O
I'm so delicious I could squeal

but would not,
never mind my false eyelashes,
my blue licorice sunglasses—
I'm so steamy it's hard

not to believe me,
not to mention the hot
apple stuffing of my voice,
the sticky gold of my hair.

nevertheless I tell you,
adjusting a chocolate and straw-
berry ice-cream tit,

I'd like to eat you up,
I've told you so before
a hundred times in writing,

sitting here on your juicy plate
like a stack of puffy pancakes

I'm not watching myself melt,
I'm not steeped in sugar and spice,
I'm not pressure cooked for nothing:

See the little round O of my mouth? Now
kiss the candy birdie:

Come, pick up your fork, slurp up
EAT ME but watch out,

* Sexy Lady Poet

163

nothing I do is true.
I'm serious, before you know it
I'll tease you into rhyme,
for the next entry in my album
I've been taking pictures of you all the time.

WHEN HE'S AT HIS MOST BRAWLING

The woman in his belly stirs.
She nudges with her armfuls of blood
The hard walls of his abdomen.
Is it her black eelgrass hair
Terrifies him?
He makes a word to evacuate her
But she knows a lot of airmail
When she hears it.
The onion skins he flies out to the world,
Full of transparent hostility,
Are not for her.
He thinks he's got her number
But deep in his hunter's body,
Tangled like a harp in his guts
She snuggles in
Like fur.
When he flexes his muscles,
Shoots off his mouth
Or gun, can't he hear her shriek
Under his hobnailed heart?
When he's at his most brawling
She's at her most brutally gentle
And all over him like a silk tent
Her shimmering laughter
Like iridescent ice-crystals
Shatters the high notes
Of his dark hysteria.

THE SLABS OF HER EYES*

The first time death struck her the criticism
Congealed her in her tracks.

Deaf as a goddess, made of lead
She simply refused to listen.

Accustomed to smiles that failed / failed
Ground down to a cold fury

And lashed to the coffin of pure self

Like a stone slab she stared in the mirror
And did not recognize herself and was not surprised.

Now, opening the door of her house like a tomb
Everyone within feeling distance shivers.

Her complexion is smooth as a lily.

Waxen, she smiles like candles
Or like the rest of us, tempted
As a flat voice sidles past us down the hall

And nobody's left but a hearing aid
Struck dumb in the middle of something unpleasant.

* On the Death of Her First Husband

MY MOTHER'S/MY/DEATH/BIRTHDAY

Now almost everything I ever imagined
Has caught up with me:
The death defying leap that worked,
The desert years that flowered,
Now the shadow has found a bed to lie down in,
I have come back from the cemetery of divorce:
Having sucked strength
From her tears, turned
Her denial into second growth
Now in my 39th year as if it were the 9th month
Heavy with summer, filled
To overflowing by the good man
She always meant me to marry,
I see him standing like an orchard
Over all the dry days of her dying:
Though the ache of her absence is the first bruise
On the blossoming plum she bore
Now even as the world descends
My mother my mold my maker
Is with me to the end:
Now the hand in the glove of the body,
The soul moves freely and well,
Pockets rolling with the stars of the one man
I always meant to love and now can.

Sylvia Plath

THE COLOSSUS

I shall never get you put together entirely,
Pieced, glued, and properly jointed.
Mule-bray, pig-grunt and bawdy cackles
Proceed from your great lips.
It's worse than a barnyard.

Perhaps you consider yourself an oracle,
Mouthpiece of the dead, or of some god or other.
Thirty years now I have labored
To dredge the silt from your throat.
I am none the wiser.

Scaling little ladders with gluepots and pails of lysol
I crawl like an ant in mourning
Over the weedy acres of your brow
To mend the immense skull plates and clear
The bald, white tumuli of your eyes.

A blue sky out of the Oresteia
Arches above us. O father, all by yourself
You are pithy and historical as the Roman Forum.
I open my lunch on a hill of black cypress.
Your fluted bones and acanthine hair are littered

In their old anarchy to the horizon-line.
It would take more than a lightning-strike
To create such a ruin.
Nights, I squat in the cornucopia
Of your left ear, out of the wind,

Counting the red stars and those of plum-color.
The sun rises under the pillar of your tongue.
My hours are married to shadow.
No longer do I listen for the scrape of a keel
On the blank stones of the landing.

MUSHROOMS

Overnight, very
Whitely, discreetly,
Very quietly

Our toes, our noses
Take hold on the loam,
Acquire the air.

Nobody sees us,
Stops us, betrays us;
The small grains make room.

Soft fists insist on
Heaving the needles,
The leafy bedding,

Even the paving.
Our hammers, our rams,
Earless and eyeless,

Perfectly voiceless,
Widen the crannies,
Shoulder through holes. We

Diet on water,
On crumbs of shadow,
Bland-mannered, asking

Little or nothing.
So many of us!
So many of us!

We are shelves, we are
Tables, we are meek,
We are edible,

Nudgers and shovers
In spite of ourselves.
Our kind multiplies:

We shall by morning
Inherit the earth.
Our foot's in the door.

BLACK ROOK IN RAINY WEATHER

On the stiff twig up there
Hunches a wet black rook
Arranging and rearranging its feathers in the rain.
I do not expect a miracle
Or an accident

To set the sight on fire
In my eye, nor seek
Any more in the desultory weather some design,
But let spotted leaves fall as they fall,
Without ceremony, or portent.

Although, I admit, I desire,
Occasionally, some backtalk
From the mute sky, I can't honestly complain:
A certain minor light may still
Leap incandescent

Out of kitchen table or chair
As if a celestial burning took
Possession of the most obtuse objects now and then—
Thus hallowing an interval
Otherwise inconsequent

By bestowing largesse, honor,
One might say love. At any rate, I now walk

Wary (for it could happen
Even in this dull, ruinous landscape); sceptical,
Yet politic; ignorant

Of whatever angel may choose to flare
Suddenly at my elbow. I only know that a rook
Ordering its black feathers can so shine
As to seize my senses, haul
My eyelids up, and grant

A brief respite from fear
Of total neutrality. With luck,
Trekking stubborn through this season
Of fatigue, I shall
Patch together a content

Of sorts. Miracles occur,
If you care to call those spasmodic
Tricks of radiance miracles. The wait's begun again,
The long wait for the angel,
For that rare, random descent.

ARIEL

Stasis in darkness.
Then the substanceless blue
Pour of tor and distances.

God's lioness,
How one we grow,
Pivot of heels and knees!—The furrow

Splits and passes, sister to
The brown arc
Of the neck I cannot catch,

172

Nigger-eye
Berries cast dark
Hooks—

Black sweet blood mouthfuls,
Shadows.
Something else

Hauls me through air—
Thighs, hair;
Flakes from my heels.

White
Godiva, I unpeel—
Dead hands, dead stringencies.

And now I
Foam to wheat, a glitter of seas.
The child's cry

Melts in the wall.
And I
Am the arrow,

The dew that flies
Suicidal, at one with the drive
Into the red

Eye, the cauldron of morning.

DADDY

You do not do, you do not do
Any more, black shoe
In which I have lived like a foot
For thirty years, poor and white,
Barely daring to breathe or Achoo.

Daddy, I have had to kill you.
You died before I had time—
Marble-heavy, a bag full of God,
Ghastly statue with one grey toe
Big as a Frisco seal

And a head in the freakish Atlantic
Where it pours bean green over blue
In the waters off beautiful Nauset.
I used to pray to recover you.
Ach, du.

In the German tongue, in the Polish town
Scraped flat by the roller
Of wars, wars, wars.
But the name of the town is common.
My Polack friend

Says there are a dozen or two.
So I never could tell where you
Put your foot, your root,
I never could talk to you.
The tongue stuck in my jaw.

It stuck in a barb wire snare.
Ich, ich, ich, ich,
I could hardly speak.
I thought every German was you.
And the language obscene

An engine, an engine
Chuffing me off like a Jew.
A Jew to Dachau, Auschwitz, Belsen.
I began to talk like a Jew.
I think I may well be a Jew.

The snows of the Tyrol, the clear beer of Vienna
Are not very pure or true.

With my gypsy ancestress and my weird luck
And my Taroc pack and my Taroc pack
I may be a bit of a Jew.

I have always been scared of *you*,
With your Luftwaffe, your gobbledygoo.
And your neat moustache
And your Aryan eye, bright blue.
Panzer-man, panzer-man, O You—

Not God but a swastika
So black no sky could squeak through.
Every woman adores a Fascist,
The boot in the face, the brute
Brute heart of a brute like you.

You stand at the blackboard, daddy,
In the picture I have of you,
A cleft in your chin instead of your foot
But no less a devil for that, no not
Any less the black man who

Bit my pretty red heart in two.
I was ten when they buried you.
At twenty I tried to die
And get back, back, back to you.
I thought even the bones would do.

But they pulled me out of the sack,
And they stuck me together with glue.
And then I knew what to do.
I made a model of you,
A man in black with a Meinkampf look

And a love of the rack and the screw.
And I said I do, I do.
So daddy, I'm finally through.

The black telephone's off at the root,
The voices just can't worm through.

If I've killed one man, I've killed two—
The vampire who said he was you
And drank my blood for a year,
Seven years, if you want to know.
Daddy, you can lie back now.

There's a stake in your fat black heart
And the villagers never liked you.
They are dancing and stamping on you.
They always *knew* it was you.
Daddy, daddy, you bastard, I'm through.

KINDNESS

Kindness glides about my house.
Dame Kindness, she is so nice!
The blue and red jewels of her rings smoke
In the windows, the mirrors
Are filling with smiles.

What is so real as the cry of a child?
A rabbit's cry may be wilder
But it has no soul.
Sugar can cure everything, so Kindness says.
Sugar is a necessary fluid,

Its crystals a little poultice.
O kindness, kindness
Sweetly picking up pieces!
My Japanese silks, desperate butterflies,
May be pinned any minute, anaesthetized.

And here you come, with a cup of tea
Wreathed in steam.

The blood jet is poetry,
There is no stopping it.
You hand me two children, two roses.

THE APPLICANT

First, are you our sort of a person?
Do you wear
A glass eye, false teeth or a crutch,
A brace or a hook,
Rubber breasts or a rubber crotch,

Stitches to show something's missing? No, no? Then
How can we give you a thing?
Stop crying.
Open your hand.
Empty? Empty. Here is a hand

To fill it and willing
To bring teacups and roll away headaches
And do whatever you tell it.
Will you marry it?
It is guaranteed

To thumb shut your eyes at the end
And dissolve of sorrow.
We make new stock from the salt.
I notice you are stark naked.
How about this suit—

Black and stiff, but not a bad fit.
Will you marry it?
It is waterproof, shatterproof, proof
Against fire and bombs through the roof.
Believe me, they'll bury you in it.

Now your head, excuse me, is empty.
I have the ticket for that.
Come here, sweetie, out of the closet.
Well, what do you think of *that?*
Naked as paper to start

But in twenty-five years she'll be silver,
In fifty, gold.
A living doll, everywhere you look.
It can sew, it can cook,
It can talk, talk, talk.

It works, there is nothing wrong with it.
You have a hole, it's a poultice.
You have an eye, it's an image.
My boy, it's your last resort.
Will you marry it, marry it, marry it.

TULIPS

The tulips are too excitable, it is winter here.
Look how white everything is, how quiet, how snowed-in.
I am learning peacefulness, lying by myself quietly
As the light lies on these white walls, this bed, these hands.
I am nobody; I have nothing to do with explosions.
I have given my name and my day-clothes up to the nurses
And my history to the anaesthetist and my body to
    surgeons.

They have propped my head between the pillow and the
    sheet-cuff
Like an eye between two white lids that will not shut.
Stupid pupil, it has to take everything in.
The nurses pass and pass, they are no trouble,
They pass the way gulls pass inland in their white caps,

Doing things with their hands, one just the same as
    another,
So it is impossible to tell how many there are.

My body is a pebble to them, they tend it as water
Tends to the pebbles it must run over, smoothing them
    gently.
They bring me numbness in their bright needles, they
    bring me sleep.
Now I have lost myself I am sick of baggage—
My patent leather overnight case like a black pillbox,
My husband and child smiling out of the family photo;
Their smiles catch onto my skin, little smiling hooks.

I have let things slip, a thirty-year-old cargo boat
Stubbornly hanging on to my name and address.
They have swabbed me clear of my loving associations.
Scared and bare on the green plastic-pillowed trolley
I watched my tea-set, my bureaus of linen, my books
Sink out of sight, and the water went over my head.
I am a nun now, I have never been so pure.

I didn't want any flowers, I only wanted
To lie with my hands turned up and be utterly empty.
How free it is, you have no idea how free—
The peacefulness is so big it dazes you,
And it asks nothing, a name tag, a few trinkets.
It is what the dead close on, finally; I imagine them
Shutting their mouths on it, like a Communion tablet.

The tulips are too red in the first place, they hurt me.
Even through the gift paper I could hear them breathe
Lightly, through their white swaddlings, like an awful
    baby.
Their redness talks to my wound, it corresponds.
They are subtle: they seem to float, though they weigh me
    down,

Upsetting me with their sudden tongues and their colour,
A dozen red lead sinkers round my neck.

Nobody watched me before, now I am watched.
The tulips turn to me, and the window behind me
Where once a day the light slowly widens and slowly thins,
And I see myself, flat, ridiculous, a cut-paper shadow
Between the eye of the sun and the eyes of the tulips,
And I have no face, I have wanted to efface myself.
The vivid tulips eat my oxygen.

Before they came the air was calm enough,
Coming and going, breath by breath, without any fuss.
Then the tulips filled it up like a loud noise.
Now the air snags and eddies round them the way a river
Snags and eddies round a sunken rust-red engine.
They concentrate my attention, that was happy
Playing and resting without committing itself.

The walls, also, seem to be warming themselves.
The tulips should be behind bars like dangerous animals;
They are opening like the mouth of some great African cat,
And I am aware of my heart: it opens and closes
Its bowl of red blooms out of sheer love of me.
The water I taste is warm and salt, like the sea,
And comes from a country far away as health.

LADY LAZARUS

I have done it again.
One year in every ten
I manage it—

A sort of walking miracle, my skin
Bright as a Nazi lampshade,
My right foot

A paperweight,
My face a featureless, fine
Jew linen.

Peel off the napkin
O my enemy.
Do I terrify?—

The nose, the eye pits, the full set of teeth?
The sour breath
Will vanish in a day.

Soon, soon the flesh
The grave cave ate will be
At home on me

And I a smiling woman.
I am only thirty.
And like the cat I have nine times to die.

This is Number Three.
What a trash
To annihilate each decade.

What a million filaments.
The peanut-crunching crowd
Shoves in to see

Them unwrap me hand and foot—
The big strip tease.
Gentleman, ladies,

These are my hands,
My knees.
I may be skin and bone,

Nevertheless, I am the same, identical woman.
The first time it happened I was ten.
It was an accident.

The second time I meant
To last it out and not come back at all.
I rocked shut

As a seashell.
They had to call and call
And pick the worms off me like sticky pearls.

Dying
Is an art, like everything else.
I do it exceptionally well.

I do it so it feels like hell.
I do it so it feels real.
I guess you could say I've a call.

It's easy enough to do it in a cell.
It's easy enough to do it and stay put.
It's the theatrical

Comeback in broad day
To the same place, the same face, the same brute
Amused shout:

"A miracle!"
That knocks me out.
There is a charge

For the eyeing of my scars, there is a charge
For the hearing of my heart—
It really goes.

And there is a charge, a very large charge,
For a word or a touch
Or a bit of blood

Or a piece of my hair or my clothes.
So, so, Herr Doktor.
So, Herr Enemy.

I am your opus,
I am your valuable,
The pure gold baby

That melts to a shriek.
I turn and burn.
Do not think I underestimate your great concern.

Ash, ash—
You poke and stir.
Flesh, bone, there is nothing there—

A cake of soap,
A wedding ring,
A gold filling.

Herr God, Herr Lucifer,
Beware
Beware.

Out of the ash
I rise with my red hair
And I eat men like air.

Marge Piercy

SIMPLE-SONG

When we are going toward someone we say
you are just like me
your thoughts are my brothers
word matches word
how easy to be together.

When we are leaving someone we say
how strange you are
we cannot communicate
we can never agree
how hard, hard and weary to be together.

We are not different nor alike
but each strange in his leather body
sealed in skin and reaching out clumsy hands
and loving is an act
that cannot outlive
the open hand
the open eye
the door in the chest standing open.

I STILL FEEL YOU

Like a fishbone in my throat
or one of your hairs that used to catch in my teeth
a piece of iron is traveling through my muscles,
a bit of jagged iron,
an end of harpoon or a broken hook.
Now it sticks as I catch my breath.
Now as I run downstairs it bites my instep.
Now it is tunneling through my belly.
It leaks a slow rust into the blood,
a sad dark orange taste on my tongue
acid but meek.
Blindly this metal remnant wanders in me

as you did, blindly taking the easiest way
in or out
whether you found an opening,
orifice or old wound,
or had to cut one.

A COLD AND MARRIED WAR

Loving you is a warm room
so I remember
how I lived on the moon.
Ash and jagged craters
cold bright place under
a black steel sky.
The stars pierced me
stabbing my secret
aches and itches.
Torture of the witch with needles.
Am I worthy, eyes?
Never. Objects
came out of the silence
bizarre as medals
for unknown services:
chocolate cherries
rolling down from Sinai,
rosebuds pink as
girls' first lipsticks.
When I lay down
head on a rock
the rock
recited tirelessly
as a language record
my sins and errors.

The months bled slowly
out of us.
The landscape went bald.

The cold stayed.
One morning there
were regulations posted.
Where I had not known
boundaries existed,
first hedges, then stakes,
finally barbed wire.
His cock crowed
I know you not,
repent, and other homilies.
My bones knocked.
Chessboard of dead volcanoes.
I had to go.

The only thing to do
with the corpse
was to eat it.

SIGN

The first white hair coils in my hand,
more wire than down or feather
Out of the bathroom mirror it glittered at me.
I plucked it, feeling thirty creep in my joints,
and found it silver. It does not melt.

My twentieth birthday lean as glass
spring vacation I stayed in the college town
twanging misery's electric banjo offkey.
I wanted to inject love right into the veins
of my thigh and wake up visible:
to vibrate color
like the minerals in stones under black light.
My best friend went home without loaning me money.
Hunger was all of the time the taste of my mouth.

Now I am ripened and sag a little from my spine.
More than most I have been the same ragged self
in all colors of luck dripping and dry,
yet love has nested in me and gradually eaten
those sense organs I used to feel with.
I have eaten my hunger soft and my ghost grows stronger.

Living in the sun so long my bones are tanned,
I am glad with my love, but everything counts now
and is counted. Gradually I am turning
to chalk, to humus, to pages and pages of paper,
to fine silver wire like something a violin
could be strung with, or somebody strung up,
or current run through: silver truly,
this hair, shiny and purposeful as forceps
if I knew how to use it.

THE ORGANIZER'S BOGEYMEN

1. *Futility*

This meeting has gone on with small interruptions
for eleven years and part of another.
I classify the speakers in small bags.
The words come out in paragraphs shaped by use.
The words stain the room like dirty water.
We all have scars.
When we stand up we show them perfunctorily.
We finger them when others speak too long.
The ten of us remaining from ten thousand
have all betrayed each other.
We come from peddling our lost future on the streets
beside Jesus Saves and stolen watches.
Every one of us is chairman in his head.
The editor of the encyclopedia of expelled factions
has deciphered a new error:
he points his knotted finger.
Then we are up and screaming like gulls

wheeling over a liner's fresh garbage.
Then we are nine.
One takes notes and applauds:
he is the agent.
I no longer remember when I first heard myself say *we*
   and mean *no one*.

2. *Prison*
The cell as coffin,
time as decay,
the self as conscious worm:
I am afraid of prison.
Alone I am a spider
run out of spit to spin with,
clinging with eight crooked legs
to a cold blank of now.
It's true walls scare me,
the man's iron routine,
the lard of boredom,
head softening inside like an overripe melon,
fingers scrabbling at salty flesh,
but my reality, my sanity
is other people.
Blindness loud as hunger hollows me.
Light breaks from the faces that I love.
I cannot live
out of that sun.

3. *Exile*
You walk through streets that itch in your nose
where children's cries are strange moths.
If you bump hard into someone
his cry is different
from your cry.
You take monthold newspapers like benzedrine
waking dry excitations
numbed in stale argument.
Every banal tourist

is a messenger from a battle
where friends
who do not remember
are impaled.
You are always a child in another language,
you are someone else.
On the sidewalks a ghostly city
is printed on the learned routine of this:
in dreams you are always back there,
in dreams you speak American.
The politics of the exile are fever,
revenge, daydream,
theater of the aging convalescent.
You wait in the wings and rehearse.
You wait and wait.

Rochelle Owens

LET US HONOR THEM, THE CLICHES WHICH HAVE GOT US ALL BY THE THROAT

I like
dead residue (a good phrase)
          it is not very cliche

but

          THE DARK RECESSES OF THE HUMAN MIND,
                    that is very cliche

the cliches are fantastically
          true, like

                    POUND IS A GREAT POET
                    THO' HE IS A FASCIST
                    Hold! Wait!
                    POUND IS A GREAT POET
                    THO' HE WAS A FASCIST
                    the old man had a
                    CHANGE OF HEART
                              ha ha
                    (note *change of heart*)
                              a big cliche

but back to THE DARK RECESSES OF THE HUMAN MIND
          it can be altered to

THE SHADOWY CREVICES OF THE HUMAN MIND
(tho' that sounds sexual, shadowy crevices)
HE PRESSED HIS FACE AGAINST HER SHADOWY CREVICES
SHADOWY CAVERNS!
that's better!

THE SHADOWY CAVERNS OF THE HUMAN MIND!
"TO CLOUD MENS MINDS"
& womens too
(that's very familiar)
WHEREBY THEY ARE CONFUSED!
ha ha a

CONFUSION OF TONGUES
Babel?
delightful?
A confusion of tongues licking
us all over
ha ha

Now that is not a cliche
neither is a polyglot of tongues
licking us all over

only a fine poet
would use

only a poet with

        polyglot of tongues

    an ear of excellence

would think up

    a polyglot of tongues

      licking

        us all over

FOR, BEHOLD THE DAY COMETH

For, Behold The Day Cometh, That
Shall Burn As An Oven; And All The
Proud, Yeah, And All That Do Wickedly,
Shall Be Stubble: And The Day That
Cometh Shall Burn Them Up, Saith The
Lord Of Hosts, That It Shall Leave Them
Neither Root Nor Branch, Yeah.

for the pentagon

Why call an anti-missile
Nike-Zeus
why not Flaming-Jesus
or Red-Eye Moses
We are a Judeo-Christian
cIvIlIzAtIoN
are we not?
               why the hang-up
                    on ancient Hellenic
                                   Gods!
                         What is it with
                                   us!
What's wrong with calling
                    a bomb
               St. Mary or
                         Big-Joel
          what's wrong with
                    Jewish names
               or Christian ones!
Are the weapons so brilliant & ruddy
like cocks
               so virile
in the eyes of the Pentagon
                         that they must
               be given
                    the names of pagan gods!

Why not Baal!
          that's a good name
or St. Luke!
            aren't they romantic enough!
Why Nike-Zeus
         why not Psalms or
                Lamentations!

THE POWER OF LOVE
HE WANTS SHIH (EVERYTHING)

First, I put my
hands on her—shou meng haou!
I'll show you.
I make my arms hard
against her softness—
she sighs . . .
her love for me
is my weapon . . .
the feeling ceases
in me . . .
& her feelings
increase . . .
her skin under
my fingers feels
like blood
not yet dry . . .
a star on fire!
& I feel wrath in me . . .
& melancholy . . . &
ice against my teeth & also
. . . . a tiny joy.

If I said to her what
was inside me . . . the words
would be . . . I will punch you . . .
to pulpwood!

The sounds I would make
would be the screams of a
vulture against
her throat.
Her mouth & legs . . . are open
. . . but my mind is working.
It's heaven's will, shua hsi!
In my mind I smear the mucus
from my nose on her breasts . . .
& drop ants into her two mouths . . .
I fill up all her orifices—
I'm very generous . . .
& she calls me the divinity
of mountains & streams &
I think of how it would be
to piss on her! She calls
herself happy & blessed &
how she feels privileged
to love me & protect me
so that I will never feel
lonely or frightened again!
I'm thinking how it
would be to throw her
into a pig-trough—
the pig slop squashing
under her buttocks &
her breasts jiggling
like rabbits!
I made her brim over
like a dark pool . . .
with my tricks—my magic!
She kept her eyes always always
on my belly, it seemed to me
as if she expected nightingales
to fly out of my belly!
& I told her stories!
Stories that I felt she must
hear!

I
   wandered
        along
with her
      in her mind
    at my own sweet will!
While
    I wandered with her
      I minced her
  into
     meatballs!
I am a magician!
         & an acrobat!
& that is enough for me!

    She is a
        mouse
      with its
      intestines
         hanging
          out
  I think she wants
        to seize me
     & grab
        & scratch
     & tickle me
inside my head is an ax
       & I cut off her head!
  What is that?
    the pigeons?

ATATURK

She'd been biting her lips lately because of the sexual tension. It was Ataturk's fault though he was the greatest she'd ever known. Was Sylvia a nympho? Not until she met him.

Sylvia had never met a Turk before. Have you? Have you? Well, Sylvia did (zowie, what a muscle-builder-combination!) at "Chock full o' nuts." What a chest he had, got it from good food & drink, what a skull shape he had, molded by a Byelorussian's! And what a quantity of energy! Very, very good. Thinking of the Philistine giant, that Turk of Sylvia's, made the inside of her thighs wet as crude sugar; faint, weak too. He was drinking a cup of coffee (the Turks brought it with them to Vienna, you know) & eating a brownie. When she sat next to him she started whiffing the harbor of Istanbul, perfume, heat-stroke, headless chickens. Sylvia smelled that man out like a mouse ripe cheese; what a fat pleasure for a girl in love . . . Sylvia fell in love right on that "Chock full o' nuts" stool & Ataturk did likewise! Sing, speak, that's what he did with his golden-brown eyes, for ten minutes! While he looked at her, while he just looked at her! She sang back at him (while the counter-people stared) her high-priestesses' membranic song. Ataturk stuffed her in his eyeballs & balanced her on his brain. A thin high squeal came out of his throat making her feel crazy.

'Ataturk's such a masculine name,' thought Sylvia. She bit her lips again, the goddamned tension. The end of her cigarette had a mixture of blood & lipstick . . . I can't tell you the sex side of their story but well, it was like the inside of a bluish lilac. 'Atagirl,' thought Sylvia. 'Very good.'

Diane Wakoski

IN GRATITUDE TO BEETHOVEN

The full roses with all their petals like the wrinkles of
    laughter
on your face as you bend to kiss someone
are bursting on the bush,
spotting my arm, as I carry a bundle of them
to my friends;
they seem to have come out of my skin
on this hot fragrant night,
and I imagine the inside of my body
glowing, phosphorescent, with strange flower faces
looking out from the duodenum
or the soft liver,
white as my belly, the eyes always disbelieving
the ugly processes that make a living body.

Here I am,
admittedly a strange combination of images;
yet constantly myself,
a funny series of animals
from the grey field mouse quietly stealing through the grain
caught by the silvery gopher snake sleekly sliding
across the grass,
caught and lifted, wriggling like a wild muscle trying to
    free itself
by the fierce open-eyed hawk,
being bitten itself by the deceptively soft tiger who will eat
    strange meat,
and is shot by the man, the hunter,
who kills for sport. Somewhere there is a consistency,
perhaps the thread of destruction,
making me a predator in every cycle
except the first one,
and I have travelled so far away from my beginnings;
no one loves me:
That I can say with certainty,

without fear of contradiction in a hundred years,
by the series of images passing,
and of course I am always
slipping through life
alone
as I am tonight,
feeling especial gratitude for Beethoven
who, in spite of all fashions,
remains a companion, whose place no one can take
permanently.
His music
has all the life you loving people I hate so much
are trying to squeeze out of me.

Yesterday I discovered I was a stingy person;
today that even my gratitudes come out of angers
at others. Who would admit as much
about himself, that he was such a failure
at creating that ultimate human good—love.

Let me say it publicly, as openly as I can,
with no delicacy or tact:
I am like the guerrilla fighter
who must sleep with one eye open for attack, a knife
or poison, a bamboo dart could come at any time.

No one has loved me without trying to destroy me,
there is no part of me that is not armoured,
there is no moment when I am not expecting attack,
there is no one I trust,
there is no love left in me that is not a wild flower,
growing at its own leisure with no cultivation period and
        no sense
of order;
one, perhaps, that only Beethoven,
now a violin or harp or piano,
could love.

(handwritten margin annotations: "looking for image of self", "nothing ever lived", "destruction of nature", "talking about herself", "on defensive")

At times, like now,
I am filled with the anger of bitterness,
a sense of having been betrayed
and then cling even more fervently to old Ludwig
whose sonatas I played for so many years
feeling
the field mouse in me slipping out through the pores in my
    skin,
running about the dusty grain field,
looking for food.
Sometimes I see my life as a cancer,
a growth with no purpose,
one that got out of hand, by some malfunctioning organ.

At times, you who look at me with so much tenderness,
you make me cry.
Where are you when I need you?
This is all literary invention, a way of
talking when there is no life.
Must it be the reality?
No one has ever moved more than the surfaces,
the images. Where is reverence
for the dialogue,
the process?
One friend tells me in the super market that I'm a
    bourgeois housewife
and won't speak to me for three hours, after my
    mentioning a
need for protein; another tells me I'm a
pushy little girl
after a conversation in which there was no agreement;
another says I'm a bad philosopher;
and another that I'm weak because I cling to a man who
    can destroy me;
but most friends tell me nothing,
are simply not there when I need them.
It is their way of dealing with the proliferation of images.

Beethoven, my gratitude for you
knows no limitations.
I keep looking for a man who will satisfactorily replace you
in my life.
That would seem to show no gratitude,
no satisfaction.
It is
in fact
only a music I have
in my ears.
A need for a similar richness.

IN PLACE OF A PHONE CALL TO ARABIA

an empty ashtray
because I don't smoke
is the mark
of something missing

the hollow
in my throat
when you can see one blue vein
like a protruding nail in a pine board
is empty too

a woman is one half of a siamese twin.
My other half/ the part
that fills the socket
of my throat
that whispers in my ear with a warm tongue
and turns my body
like an hour glass
is running empty guns in Arabia.

Sand in my mouth;
they burn it into sapphires.
You are a missing scar on my arm.

A smoked cigarette
an empty Gauloise Bleu package
I am the silver
paper
lining
it.

a feeling of emptiness

THE MAGICIAN

Your wand,
the flowering stalk of the radish,
hot,
not spicy but sharp;

I touch
with my teeth
the root,
that white bulb;

Vegetables
remind me I love you,
your transformations;

The magician works in silence.
There is no music around him, the only rhythm
a pulse in the frightened rabbit's ear.

When he folds his silks
and hangs up his suit,
he slips his baton
into his elbow.

That naked magician walks up to my doorbell
which doesn't ring.
I hear him,
the magic being now
in my ears.

He leaves his eyes on my shoulders and powdering my knees.

A POET RECOGNIZING THE ECHO OF THE VOICE

I. Isolation of Beautiful Women

> *"How were you able to get ten of the world's*
> *most beautiful women to marry you?"*
> *"I just asked them. You know, men all over*
> *the world dream about Lana Turner, desire*
> *her, want to be with her. But very very*
> *few ever ask her to marry them."*
>   —PARAPHRASE OF AN INTERVIEW WITH ARTIE SHAW

We are burning
in our heads
at night,
bonfires of our own bodies.
Persia reduces our heads
to star sapphires and lapis lazuli.
Silver threads itself
into the lines of our throats
and glitters every time we speak.
Old alchemical riddles
are solved in the dreams of men
who marry other women and think of us.
Anyone who sees us
will hold our small hands,
like mirrors in which they see themselves,
and try to initial our arms
with desperation.
Everyone wants to come close to
the cinnamon of our ears.
Every man wants to explore our bodies
and fill up our minds.
Riding their motorcycles along collapsing grey highways,
they sequester their ambivalent hunting clothes
between our legs,
reminding themselves of their value
by quoting mining stock prices, and ours.

[handwritten margin note: Men use beautiful women as outlet for fantasy a symbol - not real]

But men do not marry us,
do not ask us to share their lives,
do not survive the bonfires
hot enough to melt steel.
To alchemize rubies.

We live the loneliness
that men run after,
and we,
the precious rocks of the earth
are made harder,
more fiery
more beautiful,
more complex,
by all the pressing,
the burying,
the plundering;

even your desertions,
your betrayals,
your failure to understand and love us,
your unwillingness to face the world
as staunchly as we do;
these things
which ravage us,
cannot destroy our lives,
though they often take our bodies.
We are the earth.
We wake up
finding ourselves
glinting in the dark
after thousands of years
of pressing.

II. Movement to Establish My Identity

*I know what wages beauty gives,
How hard a life her servant lives . . .*
   —"To A Young Beauty," W. B. YEATS

A woman wakes up
finds herself
glinting in the dark;
the earth holds her
as a precious rock
in a mine

her breath is a jumble
of sediments,
of mixed strata,
of the valuable,
beautiful,
of bulk.

All men are miners;
willing to work hard
and cover themselves with pit dirt;
to dig out;
to weigh;
to possess.

Mine is a place.
Mine is a designation.
A man says, "it is mine,"
but he hacks,
chops apart the mine
to discover,
to plunder,
what's in it/ Plunder,
that is the word.
Plunder.

A woman wakes up
finds herself
scarred
but still glinting
in the dark.

III. Beauty

> *only God, my dear,*
> *Could love you for yourself alone*
> *And not your yellow hair.*
> —"For Anne Gregory," W. B. Yeats

and if I cut off my long hair,
if I stopped speaking,
if I stopped dreaming for other people about parts of the
     car,
stopped handing them tall creamy flowered silks
and loosing the magnificent hawks to fly in their direction,
stopped exciting them with the possibilities
of a thousand crystals under the fingernail
to look at while writing a letter,
if I stopped crying for the salvation of the tea ceremony,
stopped rushing in excitedly with a spikey bird-of-paradise,
and never let them see how accurate my pistol shooting is,
who would I be?

Where is the real me
I want them all to love?

We are all the textures we wear.

We frighten men with our steel;
we fascinate them with our silk;
we seduce them with our cinnamon;
we rule them with our sensuous voices;
we confuse them with our submissions.

Is there anywhere
a man
who
will not punish us
for our beauty?

He is the one
we all search for,
chanting names for exotic oceans of the moon.

He is the one
we all anticipate,
pretending these small pedestrians
jaywalking into our lives
are he.
He is the one
we all anticipate;
beauty looks for its match,
confuses the issue
with a mystery that does not exist:
the rock
that cannot burn.

We are burning
in our heads at night
the incense of our histories, finding
you have used our skulls
for ashtrays.

Margaret Atwood

GAME AFTER SUPPER

This is before electricity,
it is when there were porches.

On the sagging porch an old man
is rocking. The porch is wooden,

the house is wooden and grey;
in the living room which smells of
smoke and mildew, soon
the woman will light the kerosene lamp.

There is a barn but I am not in the barn;
there is an orchard too, gone bad,
its apples like soft cork
but I am not there either.

I am hiding in the long grass
with my two dead cousins,
the membrane grown already
across their throats.

We hear crickets and our own hearts
close to our ears;
though we giggle, we are afraid.

From the shadows around
the corner of the house
a tall man is coming to find us:

He will be an uncle,
if we are lucky.

STORIES IN KINSMAN'S PARK

We take the children to the park
where there are swings,
a wading pool;

their father is in the hospital,
the latest scar contracting
across his scalp.

When they are tired of water
and climbing, we tell stories,
making witches from coloured wool.

> In the sun all wounds
> are imaginary or cured
> by secret leaves, the green place
> expands around us, holds us
> enclosed, the high
> voices of children immerse
> us, quick and continuous as insects
>
> Here, we are convinced
> death can occur only
> to witches and in
> the sanctioned ways. The victorious
> children live, as they should,
> in the forest forever.
>
> Cars start; the day re-enters
> us, the pool water is gone
> before we notice.
>
> Driving for home,
> the older one wants to know
> how to stop thunder;
> he says he is afraid of things
> that get in through the windows.

The younger says
he is afraid of nothing;
he is the one who wants

the light on, who has
bad dreams, the caterpillar
eating the side of his head.

IT IS DANGEROUS TO READ NEWSPAPERS

While I was building neat
castles in the sandbox,
the hasty pits were
filling with bulldozed corpses

and as I walked to the school
washed and combed, my feet
stepping on the cracks in the cement
detonated red bombs.

Now I am grownup
and literate, and I sit in my chair
as quietly as a fuse

and the jungles are flaming, the under-
brush is charged with soldiers,
the names on the difficult
maps go up in smoke.

I am the cause, I am a stockpile of chemical
toys, my body
is a deadly gadget,
I reach out in love, my hands are guns,
my good intentions are completely lethal.

Even my
passive eyes transmute

everything I look at to the pocked
black and white of a war photo,
how
can I stop myself

It is dangerous to read newspapers.

Each time I hit a key
on my electric typewriter,
speaking of peaceful trees

another village explodes.

THE LANDLADY

This is the lair of the landlady.

She is
a raw voice
loose in the rooms beneath me,

the continuous henyard
squabble going on below
thought in this house like
the bicker of blood through the head.

She is everywhere, intrusive as the smells
that bulge in under my doorsill;
she presides over my
meagre eating, generates
the light for eyestrain.

From her I rent my time:
she slams
my days like doors.
Nothing is mine

and when I dream images
of daring escapes through the snow
I find myself walking
always over a vast face
which is the land-
lady's, and wake up shouting.

She is a bulk, a knot
swollen in space. Though I have tried
to find some way around
her, my senses
are cluttered by perception
and can't see through her.

She stands there, a raucous fact
blocking my way:
immutable, a slab
of what is real,

solid as bacon.

MIDWINTER, PRESOLSTICE

The cold rises around
our house, the wind
drives through the walls in
splinters; on the inside
of the window, behind
the blanket we have hung
a white mould thickens.

We spend the days quietly
trying to be warm; we can't
look through the glass;
in the refrigerator old food
sickens, gives out.

I dream of departures, meetings,
repeated weddings with a stranger, wounded
with knives and bandaged, his
face hidden

       All night my gentle husband
sits alone in the corner
of a grey arena, guarding
a paper bag
       which holds
turnips and apples and my
head, the eyes closed

THE REVENANT

The child's face at the window
the twisted child's face

its fingers scratching
against the glass, against
the clinical ice

Vindictive
child, playing in your
interminable gardens, whispering
behind me always your dwarf
resentments, tugging my nerves towards
your boring predictable joys,

writing your own name
over and over in the snow

Mirror addict, my sickness
how can I get rid of you.

You don't exist.

The child, its face twisted
with tears, going
barefoot in thorny winter,
wrists bleeding, a frozen martyr

the white tyrant, crowned
and sullen in those green indelible
forests, that vague
province, vast as a hospital

the skull's noplace, where in me
refusing to be buried, cured,
the trite dead walk.

THEY EAT OUT

In restaurants we argue
over which of us will pay for your funeral

though the real question is
whether or not I will make you immortal.

At the moment only I
can do it and so

I raise the magic fork
over the plate of beef fried rice

and plunge it into your heart.
There is a faint pop, a sizzle

and through your own split head
you rise up glowing;

the ceiling opens
a voice sings Love Is A Many

Splendoured Thing
you hang suspended above the city

in blue tights and a red cape,
your eyes flashing in unison.

The other diners regard you
some with awe, some only with boredom:

they cannot decide if you are a new weapon
or only a new advertisement.

As for me, I continue eating;
I liked you better the way you were,
but you were always ambitious.

THEIR ATTITUDES DIFFER

1
To understand
each other: anything
but that, & to avoid it

I will suspend my search for
germs if you will keep
your fingers off the microfilm
hidden inside my skin

2
I approach this love
like a biologist
pulling on my rubber
gloves & white labcoat

You flee from it
like an escaped political
prisoner, and no wonder

3
You held out your hand
I took your fingerprints

You asked for love
I gave you only descriptions

Please die I said
so I can write about it

AFTER ALL YOU ARE QUITE

After all you are quite
ordinary: 2 arms 2 legs
a head, a reasonable
body, toes & fingers, a few
eccentricities, a few honesties
but not too many, too many
postponements & regrets but

you'll adjust to it, meeting
deadlines and other
people, pretending to love
the wrong woman some of the
time, listening to your brain
shrink, your diaries
expanding as you grow older,

growing older, of course you'll
die but not yet, you'll outlive
even my distortions of you

and there isn't anything
I want to do about the fact
that you are unhappy & sick

you aren't sick & unhappy
only alive & stuck with it.

Lyn Lifshin

TO POEM

all night
you banged
in my head
poking your fingers
thru me, hot for
blood and then
in the morning
stretching out on
the table
flaunting your muscles
when you knew there wasn't time.
Later in the car
you made me dizzy.
but worse, how you
made my love jealous
perching in my hair
with those stiff wings.
and now, bastard
alone with me finally
the chance to
scares you off

IN SPITE OF HIS DANGLING PRONOUN

He was really her favorite
student dark and just
back from the army with
hot olive eyes, telling her of
bars and the first
time he got a piece of
ass in Greece or was it
Italy and drunk on some strange
wine and she thought
in spite of his dangling

pronoun (being twenty four and
never screwed but in her
soft nougat thighs) that he
would be a
lovely experience.
So she shaved her legs up high
and when he came
talking of footnotes she
locked him tight in her
snug black file cabinet where
she fed him twice a day and
hardly anyone noticed
how they lived among bluebooks
in the windowless office
rarely coming up for sun or the
change in his pronoun or the
rusty creaking chair
or that many years later
they were still going to town in
novels she never had time to finish

FOR A FRIEND

Leaving beer and apples
on the window
for later
lying together those nights
till four,
talking
everybody must have thought
that we were
lovers
your red mustache in the blanket
smell of your cigarette in my hair
white thighs in the mountains
getting bombed on the sky

But when I stand
back I don't recognize
myself or
you love
who got into my skirt
and blood
before I knew
your name and then
wanted to be
mostly friends

Those 3 weeks
everything that moved in my
bones stretched
toward you,

I wanted to take you inside me that deep
your crooked smile, Russian
eyes but you
grew into the desk, your
back a wall

What were
you feeling those
nights we undressed, then
in the dark
you asked who else I could
talk to like this
while I was wondering what to do
with feelings I
couldn't use,
your face
so close to mine
it chilled me

NICE

floating thru chairs
then opening
your hand
snakes in thru corduroy
my slip rides up the sun
makes the rug into a wool beach
sand   assapples   a wave of
thighs opening
skin prints a v on the rug your
knees go there
opening
and mouths suddenly too a
crack touch the pink smell
the sleek breathing flesh moans
a taste is nipples
bumping and your sail of blood
shove of bone tongue
travelling into this moist
lips opening the first bang of
hair and clothes rise from bodies
tremble the warm buttons rubbing
scratch of your mouth there
the damp nylon crotch
petals dissolving in a water my silk
hips you open and your fingers
under plunge so are pressing lips there
and your flesh
root shining
rocks your heat to my belly and my
legs spread so wide
greedy for the whole boat of you
in me your lovejuice dipping these
sloppy hills of cunt and you
put your good
hardness up me   opening

skin rooms pounding
and circles slide your raw stem
my nails pull you
tighter
in and the slap of licked flesh oil
waves lunging and teeth
that eat everywhere ramming
the slit wet
opening and spread so
wide and splitting bite the sweet hot ache swell
your bomb breaking
too sucks the whole room up
fur zippersbeercans
and the sweat hair of groaning and sperm
till your cock bud throbs more
to ball me over and
again   better than summer
deep and nice
bringing everything
home

DOWNSTAIRS TWO OLD LOVERS MEET AND (?) TALK ABOUT ME

it's not that
unlikely that
we're meeting
in this place

with our words
in our suitcases

i can hear them
talking saying
what i did
with my tongue

233

sweaty   in a
room over them
listening

But this is
a lie   i wanted
to imagine

things they'd say
as tho it would
make them mean
more than
their bodies

Yes my skin
burned when i
saw them both
tonight   but

it was the way
wind ripples a
dead animal's fur
and what happens
seems to come
from inside

WOMEN LIKE THAT

Usually they
go, women like that
because if they

stay nothing
sleeps right. Stones
and chairs

float above the onions
and the husband
has trouble

knowing what to do.
There's always a little
winter in their house

If there are
children they touch her
snow cautiously like they

might a pretty glass
witch. And because of this,
maybe   these   women

press their eyes, close
them down so hard
they make

their own purple light
and afternoons flow into
the weeds of a

flimsy lover's hair.
Or look away
far off to a place so far

away it can't
matter. Then they come back
and write lies about it

THE BLUE BOWL OF PLUMS INVENTION
OR, NOT TILL THE

night his
house i don't remember

when i saw him in the
car with,
had he married her
red hair   Wait
it's a dream i wanted to
yell   how could you
do it after what

and we went upstairs
she was teaching   i had to
think of
time the
clock   i can't
stand it i'm sobbing
pulling on the
sheets

and he shows me letters
written all july and
never mailed   i
would have answered
(a lie except for the
blue bowl of plums,
the way the
shade moves)

we might have
made love because i think
of getting dressed still
crying how

and he put his head down
on the table
but really he loved
seeing me this
way   even my
legs felt sweaty

236

two cats howled   i
knew we couldn't
go on,

that i'd have to be
famous instead

Erica Jong

AGING

(balm for a 27th birthday)

Hooked for two years now on wrinkle creams   creams for
crowsfeet   ugly lines (if only there were one!)
any perfumed grease   which promises   youth   beauty
not truth   but all I need on earth
              I've been studying   how women age

                                             how

it starts around the eyes   so you can tell
a woman of 22 from one of 28 merely by
a faint scribbling near the lids   a subtle crinkle
          a fine line
extending from the fields of vision

                                             this

in itself is not unbeautiful   promising
              as it often does
insights which clear-eyed 22 has no inkling of
promising   certain sure-thighed things in bed
certain fingers on your spine & lids

                                             but

it's only the beginning   as ruin proceeds downward
lingering for a while around the mouth   hardening the
          smile
into prearranged patterns (irreversible!)   writing furrows
from the wings of the nose   (oh nothing much at first
              but "showing promise"   like your early poems

                                             of deepening)

& plotting lower to the corners of the mouth   drooping
          them

a little ˈ like the tragic mask   though not at all grotesque
as yet ˌ& then as you sidestep   into the 4th decade
beginning to crease the neck   (just slightly)
        though the breasts below

                                        especially

when they're small (like mine) may stay high far
            into the thirties
still the neck will give you away   & after that the chin
which   though you may snip it back & hike it up under
your earlobes will never quite love your bones as it once
        did

                                        though

the belly may be kept firm through numerous pregnancies
by means of sit-ups   jogging   dancing   (think of Russian
        ballerinas)
        & the cunt
as far I know is ageless   possibly immortal   becoming
        simply
more open   more quick to understand   more dry-eyed
        than at 22

                                        which

after all   is what you were dying for   (as you ravaged
islands of turtles   beehives   oysterbeds   the udders of
        cows)
desperate to censor changes which you simply might have
        let play
over you   lying back   listening   opening yourself
        letting the years make love the only way   (poor
            blunderers)

                                        they know

242

BITTER PILLS FOR THE DARK LADIES

"—hardly a person at all, or a woman,
certainly not another 'poetess,' but. . ."
—Robert Lowell about Sylvia Plath

If you've got to   if after trying to
give it up (like smoking or Nembutal)
if after swearing to   shut it up   it keeps on
yakking (that voice in your head)
that insomniac who lives across the wall,
that amateur Hammondist
who plays those broken scales next door
o then   consider yourself doomed to.

Ambition bites. Bite back.
(It's almost useless.) Suppose yourself born
half black, half Jewish in Missis-
sippi, & with one leg
                    You get the Idear?
Jus' remember you got no rights. Anything go wrong
they gonna roun' you up & howl "Poetess!"
(sorta like "Nigra!") then kick the shit outa you
sayin': You got Natural Rhythm (28 days)
so why you wanna mess aroun'?

Words bein' slippery & poetry bein'
mos'ly a matter of balls,
men what gives in to the lilt and lift of words
(o love   o death   o organ tones   o dickey!)
is "Cosmic." You is "Sentimental."
So dance in your Master's bed (or thesis) & shut
yo' mouth. Ain't you happiest there?

If they let you out   it's as Supermansaint
played by S. Poitier   with Ph.D.[2]   & a buttondown fly
washed whiter than any other on the block.
& the ultimate praise is always a question of nots:

243

                    viz. not a like woman
                    viz. "certainly not another 'poetess' "

meanin'

          she got a cunt but she don't talk funny
          & he's a nigger but he don't smell funny

& the only good poetess is a dead.

Nikki Giovanni

FOR SAUNDRA

i wanted to write
a poem
that rhymes
but revolution doesn't lend
itself to be-bopping

then my neighbor
who thinks i hate
asked—do you ever write
tree poems—i like trees
so i thought
i'll write a beautiful green tree poem
peeked from my window
to check the image
noticed the school yard was covered
with asphalt
no green—no trees grow
in manhattan

then, well, i thought the sky
i'll do a big blue sky poem
but all the clouds have winged
low since no-Dick was elected

so i thought again
and it occurred to me
maybe i shouldn't write
at all
but clean my gun
and check my kerosene supply

perhaps these are not poetic
times
at all

BLACK POWER

(For All the Beautiful Black Panthers East)

But the whole thing is a miracle—See?

We were just standing there
talking—not touching or smoking
Pot
When this cop told
Tyrone
Move along buddy—take your whores
outa here

And this tremendous growl
From out of nowhere
Pounced on him

Nobody to this very day
Can explain
How it happened

And none of the zoos or circuses
Within fifty miles
Had reported
A panther
Missing

WOMAN POEM

you see, my whole life
is tied up
to unhappiness
its father cooking breakfast
and me getting fat as a hog
or having no food
at all and father proving

his incompetence
again
i wish i knew how it would feel
to be free

its having a job
they won't let you work
or no work at all
castrating me
(yes it happens to women too)

its a sex object if you're pretty
and no love
or love and no sex if you're fat
get back fat black woman be a mother
grandmother strong thing but not woman
gameswoman romantic woman love needer
man seeker dick eater sweat getter
fuck needing love seeking woman

its a hole in your shoe
and buying lil sis a dress
and her saying you shouldn't
when you know
all too well—that you shouldn't

but smiles are only something we give
to properly dressed social workers
not each other
only smiles of i know
your game sister
which isn't really
a smile

joy is finding a pregnant roach
and squashing it
not finding someone to hold
let go get off get back don't turn

me on you black dog
how dare you care
about me
you ain't got no good sense
cause i ain't shit you must be lower
than that to care

its a filthy house
with yesterday's watermelon
and monday's tears
cause true ladies don't
know how to clean

its intellectual devastation
of everybody
to avoid emotional commitment
"yeah honey i would've married
him but he didn't have no degree"

its knock-kneed mini skirted
wig wearing died blond mamma's scar
born dead my scorn your whore
rough heeled broken nailed powdered
face me
whose whole life is tied
up to unhappiness
cause its the only
for real thing
i
know

BIOGRAPHIES

MARGARET ATWOOD (*born 1939 in Ottawa, Canada*) says, "My life really has been writing since the age of sixteen; all other decisions I made were determined by that fact." She has lived all over Canada as well as in the U.S. and England. Her books of poems include *The Circle Game* (1966), *The Animals In That Country* (1968), *The Journals of Susanna Moodie* and *Procedures For Underground* (1970), and *Power Politics* (1971). She has also published two novels: *The Edible Woman* (1970) and *Surfacing* (1972).

BESMILR BRIGHAM (*born 1923 in Pace, Mississippi*) is descended from a Choctaw. She has lived in the Southwest, Mexico, Alaska, Canada, France, and Nicaragua, and now resides on a farm in Horatio, Arkansas. She studied at the New School for Social Research in the late 1950's, but did not begin publishing until 1966. Her work includes *Agony Dance: Death of the Dancing Dolls* (1969) and *Heaved From the Earth* (1971).

GWENDOLYN BROOKS (*born 1917 in Topeka, Kansas*) is the first black woman to win the Pulitzer Prize for poetry, for her second volume of poems, *Annie Allen*, in 1950. She resides in Chicago, where for years she has pursued her special interest: encouraging young black creative talent. Other works include a novel, *Maud Martha* (1953), *Bronzeville Boys and Girls* (1956),

In the Mecca (1968), *Riot* (1970), and the autobiography, *Report from Part One* (1972). Her writing has been collected in *The World of Gwendolyn Brooks* (1971).

EMILY DICKINSON (*born 1830 in Amherst, Massachusetts*), except for a few brief excursions into the world, lived all her life in the house where she was born; she died there in 1886. For the last twenty years of her life she rarely ventured beyond her garden gate, saw no one but her family and a few friends, dressed always in white, and wrote more than 1775 poems on scraps of paper which she tied with thread and thrust into bureau drawers. The definitive editions of her works, edited by T. H. Johnson, are *Letters* (1958) and *Complete Poems* (1960).

MARI EVANS (*a native of Toledo, Ohio*) is producer/director of a weekly television series, *The Black Experience*, and is Writer-in-Residence and Assistant Professor of Black Literature at Indiana University. Her volume, *I Am A Black Woman*, received the Indiana University Writers' Conference Award for the most distinguished work of poetry by an Indiana author in 1970, and the Black Academy of Arts and Letters First Annual Poetry Award in 1971.

NIKKI GIOVANNI (*born 1943*) has recently completed her autobiography, *Gemini* (which is also her sign). She is the author of *Black Judgement* (1968), *Black Feeling, Black Talk* (1970), and *Spin A Soft Black Song: Poems for Children* (1971). Her latest book of poems is titled *My House* (1972).

PATRICIA GOEDICKE (*born 1931 in Boston, Massachusetts*) received a National Endowment of the Arts Award for her first book of poems, *Between Oceans* (1968). She was graduated from Middlebury College and spent several years working and writing in New York City. She has been a lecturer in English at Ohio University and Hunter College and now teaches poetry at the Instituto Allende in San Miguel de Allende, Mexico. She is now working on her fourth book, tentatively titled, *I Wanted You To Make Love To Me and You Did, Baby, You Did.*

ERICA JONG (*born 1942*) lives and writes in New York City, where she teaches a poetry-writing workshop at the 92nd Street Y. She was educated at Barnard and Columbia and was a college instructor of English for a while. Her first book of poems, *Fruits & Vegetables* appeared in 1971. A second volume, *Half-Lives*, was published in the spring of 1973; and a novel, *Fear of Flying*, is due to be published in late 1973.

CAROLYN KIZER (*born 1925 in Spokane, Washington*) was one of the founding editors of *Poetry Northwest*. She attended Sarah Lawrence College and Columbia University and in 1967 was appointed Poet-in-Residence at the University of North Carolina. She is currently director of the Graduate Writing Program at Columbia. Her published books include *The Ungrateful Garden* (1961), *Knock Upon Silence* (1965), and *And Midnight Was My Cry* (1971).

DENISE LEVERTOV (*born 1923 in London, came to the U.S. in 1948*) is currently involved in the Ad Hoc Leaflet Collective, Brookline Citizens for a General Strike, Resist, and other political organizations. She has lived in New York, Maine, and Mexico and now resides in the Boston area with her husband, Mitchell Goodman. She has also been a Visiting Professor or Poet-in-Residence at Vassar, CCNY, Berkeley, and MIT. Her volumes of poetry include *With Eyes at the Back of Our Heads* (1960), *The Jacob's Ladder* (1961), *O Taste and See* (1964), *The Sorrow Dance* (1967), *Relearning the Alphabet* (1970), *To Stay Alive* (1971), and *Footprints* (1972).

LYN LIFSHIN has attended Yaddo and won the Harcourt Brace fellowship to the Boulder Writers' Conference. She received her B.A. from Syracuse and her M.A. from the University of Vermont. She is presently living and writing in Albany. Some of her published works are *Why Is the House Dissolving* (1968) and *Black Apples*

(1971). Crossing Press is planning to bring out a volume of her collected poems in the near future.

MARIANNE MOORE (*born 1887 in St. Louis, granddaughter of a Presbyterian minister*) was active into her old age as poet, reviewer, and translator. Retaining her enthusiams for life and the Brooklyn Dodgers, she became a well-known personality about New York. She was educated at Bryn Mawr and from 1921 on lived with her mother in New York City. She was an assistant in the New York Public Library and later an editor of *Dial* magazine. The unofficial poet laureatess of America died in 1972. The last edition of her work is the *Complete Poems* (1967).

ROCHELLE OWENS (*born 1936*) is well known as a playwright, particularly for *Futz*, which won an Obie in 1968. Other plays include *Beclch* and *Kontraption. He Wants Shih!* and a musical, *The Karl Marx Play*, are scheduled for world premieres. She has edited an anthology of new American plays, *Spontaneous Combustion Plays*, and is a founding member of The New York Theatre Strategy and The Women's Theatre Council. She has published three other books of poetry in addition to *Salt and Core* (1968).

MARGE PIERCY (*born 1936*) lives in Wellfleet on Cape Cod "in an open relationship with a man I've been with for ten years and another who comes and goes; and a lot of people who pass time here." She is active in new-left politics and is presently engaged in building a women's movement on the East Coast. She has published three novels: *Going Down Fast* (1969), *Dance the Eagle to Sleep* (1970), and *Small Changes* (1972), as well as three books of poems: *Breaking Camp* (1968), *Hard Loving* (1969), and *4-Telling* (1970).

SYLVIA PLATH (*born 1932 in Boston*) was a brilliant graduate of Smith College and a Fulbright scholar at Cambridge. She taught at Smith and then moved permanently to England with her husband, British poet Ted Hughes. When she was thirty years old, she com-

presently Visiting Professor of Creative Literature at Brandeis University. She was graduated from Radcliffe College and from 1953 to 1966 lived in Cambridge, Massachusetts, married, and had three sons. She has also taught at Swarthmore, Columbia, and City College. She has published seven books of poetry: *A Change of World* (1951), *The Diamond Cutters* (1955), *Snapshots of a Daughter-in-Law* (1963), *Necessities of Life* (1966), *Leaflets* (1969), *The Will to Change* (1971), and *Diving Into the Wreck* (1973).

ANNE SEXTON (*born 1928 in Newton, Massachusetts*) was awarded the Pulitzer Prize for her book *Live or Die*. She claims she was "reborn in Newton, Mass., in 1957 when [she] started to write," and has for most of her life resided within a five-mile range of Newton. She is married, has two daughters, and has published six books of poetry: *To Bedlam and Part Way Back* (1960), *All My Pretty Ones* (1962), *Live or Die* (1966), *Love Poems* (1967), *Transformations* (1971) and *The Book of Folly* (1972). She is at present working simultaneously on three books and is teaching creative writing at Boston University. She says, "Life is exciting for me. Long live the word!"

MAY SWENSON (*born 1919 in Logan, Utah, of Swedish Mormon immigrant parents*) was elected a member of the National Institute of Arts and Letters in 1970. She has been Poet-in-Residence at Purdue, University of North Carolina, and Utah State University but has spent her writing career mainly in and around New York City. Her volumes of poetry are *To Mix With Time* (1963), *Half Sun Half Sleep* (1967), *Poems to Solve* (1969), *More Poems to Solve* (1970), and *Iconographs* (1970).

PS589
S4

C34116

JUL 2 6 1

Segnitz, Barbara, 1936–   comp.
    Psyche: the feminine poetic consciousness; an an
of modern American women poets, edited by Barba
nitz and Carol Rainey. ₁New York₁ Dial Press, :

    256 p. 21 cm. $10.00

    1. Women's writings, American. 2. American poetry—
tury.   I. Rainey, Carol, 1942–   joint comp. II. Title.

PS589.S4   811'.5'08   7
ISBN 0-8037-7207-6

Library of Congress   74 ₁4₁

Please Do Not Remove Card From Pocket

YOUR LIBRARY CARD

may be used at all library agencies. You
are, of course, responsible for all materials
checked out on it. As a courtesy to others
please return materials promptly — before
overdue penalties are imposed.

The SAINT PAUL PUBLIC LIBRARY